MYTH BUSTING ECONOMICS

MYTH BUSTING ECONOMICS

A NO-NONSENSE GUIDE TO YOUR MONEY, YOUR BUSINESS AND THE AUSTRALIAN ECONOMY

STEPHEN KOUKOULAS

WILEY

First published in 2015 by John Wiley & Sons Australia, Ltd
42 McDougall St, Milton Qld 4064
Office also in Melbourne

Typeset in 11/13.5 pt ITC Giovanni Std by Aptara, India

National Library of Australia Cataloguing-in-Publication data:

Creator:	Koukoulas, Stephen, author.
Title:	Myth-busting economics: a no-nonsense guide to your money, your business and the Australian economy / Stephen Koukoulas.
ISBN:	9780730321958 (pbk.) 9780730321965 (ebook)
Notes:	Includes index.
Subjects:	Financial literacy—Australia. Finance, Personal—Australia. Economics—Australia—Popular works.
Dewey Number:	332.024

Cover design by Wiley

Cover image © GoodLifeStudio/iStockphoto.com

Printed in Australia by Ligare Book Printer

10 9 8 7 6 5 4 3 2 1

Disclaimer
The material in this publication is of the nature of general comment only, and does not represent professional advice. It is not intended to provide specific guidance for particular circumstances and it should not be relied on as the basis for any decision to take action or not take action on any matter which it covers. Readers should obtain professional advice where appropriate, before making any such decision. To the maximum extent permitted by law, the author and publisher disclaim all responsibility and liability to any person, arising directly or indirectly from any person taking or not taking action based on the information in this publication.

CONTENTS

ABOUT THE AUTHOR

Stephen Koukoulas is one of Australia's leading economic visionaries. With his rare and specialised professional experience from almost 30 years as an economist, he looks at economics with refreshing honesty and openness, especially when the answer to many of the economic issues of the day are neither black nor white.

His first job was in the Commonwealth Treasury in Canberra, arriving in an office where most of the staff were smoking, ashtrays were overflowing, the floor was a Soviet-grey lino and there was a huge computer printout of data on his desk that had to be checked with a sharp pencil and a calculator. After 8 years, Stephen moved to Citibank in Sydney and, at age 33, was appointed Chief Economist. It was in this role where he started to gain a profile in the business sector, funds management industry and the media. But in 1999, when Citibank merged with Salomon Smith Barney, Stephen was left to 'look for other opportunities in the market'; in other words made redundant as the new Citibank strove for new 'synergies' and 'efficiencies'. The 'other opportunities' for Stephen came in the form of a writing role at *The Australian Financial Review*. It was here that he started to stir the pot with frank and fearless analysis, opinion articles and bold calls in the financial markets.

The years that follow see Stephen returning to the financial markets, working for TD Securities which led to a promotion that would take him to London just before the global financial crisis. It might have been this experience that formed Stephen's views about the virtues of using all levers of policy to promote economic growth and preserve jobs in times of economic and market upheaval.

On returning to Australia in 2010, he rejoined Treasury part-time as the macroeconomic adviser on financial markets. With the GFC still bubbling along in one form or another, he worked with then

Treasurer Wayne Swan's office up on Capital Hill, talking through and analysing what the high Aussie dollar, the Greek debt disaster and the still fractured markets might mean for policy settings in Australia. A few months later, the 2010 election saw the return of the Gillard government and Stephen's mate, Jim Chalmers, who was Chief of Staff to Treasurer Wayne Swan and is now the Federal Member for Rankin, asked him if he would like to be economic policy adviser to Prime Minister Julia Gillard.

Stephen was in Prime Minister Gillard's office for 10 months before leaving for personal reasons. In 2011, Stephen established his own advisory business, Market Economics, which prepares independent and tailored macroeconomic analysis for business clients needing to convert economic data into financial market and policy risks. His work provides clients with interesting and often unique insights into the macroeconomic policy debate.

With his unique background and knowledge, Stephen offers more than many economists. He has briefed Australian Prime Minister Tony Abbott on crucial economic policy issues; presented to over 35 central banks around the world; and delivered keynote addresses to the corporate world, the small business sector, retail investors and even Year 12 HSC economics students. He is a popular talking head for the ABC, Sky TV, radio and Network Ten's *The Project*, and has a reputation for breaking down complex issues on the economy into easily understood commentary and analysis of the matter at hand.

For more on Stephen, or to follow his blog, visit www.thekouk.com.

ACKNOWLEDGEMENTS

For Meredith, oh how I miss you.

To Phoebe and Oskar — the shining lights of my life.

This, my first book, was sparked by some colourful conversations with the wonderful people from Ode Management, a speaker management office, or as they call themselves, 'a direct management office for some of the world's greatest disruptors, innovators and thought leaders'. I am reluctant to single anyone out for fear of missing someone but the infectious enthusiasm of Leanne Christie, Julie Masters, Lauren Kelly, Heidi Gregory, Fiona Pascoe and Darren Reid deserves a mention. They were the catalyst for getting many of the things I speak to clients about into this book.

Then there were the people at my publisher, Wiley — patient people as I stumbled through the process of working out what to do. And here is the finished product. So thanks to Chris Shorten, Jem Bates, Ingrid Bond and Lucy Raymond.

I would also like to thank Alan Kohler for allowing me to use some of the material from *Business Spectator* and for being an all-round good bloke.

And of course, to those over the years who have nurtured and fine-tuned my career and ideas on economics and financial markets and on how to sell a story. The likes of Grant Bailey, Chris Pashley, Mark Aldridge, Colleen Ryan, Roger Kilham, Martine Irman and from the distant past, it now seems, Chris Higgins, are just a few of the special people that probably don't realise how much they influenced my career. What good people they are. To Arthur Sinodinos, thanks for hiring me as a graduate in Treasury all those years ago.

Finally, to my family. The last few years have taught me more about life than I will ever know about economics. More than I wanted to know. Who cares where the economy is or where interest rates are going when your world falls apart. Loved ones matter, not the ASX200. There is the personal exhilaration so often experienced in life and shared with your family during the good times, usually when luck also goes your way. These feelings are best shared and should be savoured like there is no tomorrow. Alas, we have also had to share the horrid grief and absolute despondency when ill-health and death end the most special relationships.

PREFACE

I adore economics and financial markets. They incorporate so much that is good for people, and for social fairness and decency, when implemented well. Yet there is a dark side that can be, and often is, exploited so these economic gains are eroded, unrealised or unequally distributed in society.

I am lucky to have spent all of my professional career tied up in real-world economics. That means I have applied the economic theory I first learned 30 years ago when studying for my honours degree in economics at the Australian National University.

While the learning process in economics and markets never really ends as long as your mind remains open to new ideas, many of the fundamental underpinnings of economics and finance will always hold true. Whether I am talking to a fund manager in Boston, Dubai or Beijing with many billions of dollar to invest, a Year 12 Higher School Certificate student in Canberra or Sydney, or people in the mortgage industry, or advising the prime minister or treasurer or the head of Treasury, the key issues of growth, sustainability, fairness, risk management and scenario planning are much the same.

Economics is not that hard, so long as you are aware of the linkages and consequences of acting in one area or another. Being alert to why government economic policy is changing or should change is enriching, even if it is simply to crystallise your thoughts on why some changes are inadvisable. I have long been shocked by how few people carefully audit their personal finances, especially at a time when the government is focused on cutting spending and raising taxes. As we get older we need to be sure we will have enough money to live comfortably in retirement, with decent health care and the financial freedom to do nice things, for ourselves and our children.

The importance of economic policy matters is matched by their frequent coverage in the media. Whether I'm giving a quick interview for a news grab on Radio 2GB, having a longer chat on the ABC's Radio National or doing a spot on *The Project* or Sky Business TV, I have found that the thirst for information in the media is constant.

At a personal level, and this is really the pitch of this book, economics covers your job, business and superannuation. It spans interest rates, buying a racehorse, reverse mortgages and gap years for young adults, and so much more. It's about being aware of the economic policy our political leaders deliver and making sure we know what is at stake economically when we elect this or that government. And don't forget about the rest of the world and its pivotal influence on the Australian economy, which of course means you.

If you gain nothing else from reading this book, I hope you will be alerted to the importance of monitoring your own personal finances, from the fees you pay on your mortgage and superannuation to the costs of owning a dog or going to the theatre. Economics is about making choices. Some of the money you spend on buying that morning coffee might instead contribute to paying off your debt.

By the end of the book, I hope you will be more aware of your financial position and have a better sense of the trade-offs involved in spending today rather than saving or investing for tomorrow. I also hope you are encouraged to participate actively in the national economic debate and thereby help guide Australia towards better policy choices and better economic outcomes. Be informed and aware about economics and money, and be vocal. After all, at the end of the day it is all about you.

chapter one MASTERCHEF VS MASTER ECONOMIST

My motivations for writing this book include frustration and disappointment with the direction of national economic policy, the prevailing lack of financial self-awareness and the woeful state of financial planning in Australia. The reality is that many people have little understanding of their own financial status, let alone the high-brow economic policy contemplated and delivered by the government of the day. An equally worrying problem is the unhelpful and often counterproductive financial advice given to business, mortgage holders and those saving for retirement through their superannuation fund. This may sound like a harsh assessment, but as you work your way through the following pages, there should be a realisation that this assessment is correct: people are complacent when it comes to their own money and the big-picture policy settings that influence their financial wellbeing.

The problem of financial complacency

I'll start by noting that many Australians simply don't care about politics and, by default, economic policy. This is demonstrated by Australian Electoral Commission estimates that show some 10 per cent of eligible voters do not bother to register on the electoral roll. A further 10 per cent of people on the electoral roll don't turn up to vote at each election. Add to that a further 5 per cent or more who cast an informal vote. On top of all this, an unknown number register a formal vote only because they are required to and would be fined if they failed to do so. Despite this level of apathy, there are unending complaints from the community about the government of the day, whether Labor or Liberal/National Party Coalition. 'They are all hopeless!' is the all too common refrain. And often at the core of these complaints are the government's economic policies, whether implemented or merely promised.

This level of disengagement encourages politicians to pitch the economic policy debate at simple, hip pocket issues that voters are most likely to fasten on when they watch the 10- or 20-second grab on the evening news. Major economic policy reforms that set Australia up so well in decades past were debated, analysed and implemented for the medium- to long-run wellbeing of the economy, rather than being advocated and shot down in the interests of political point scoring, as is all too frequently the case now.

As for people being aware of their own finances, an Essential Research poll conducted in 2014 found that 52 per cent of people with superannuation savings paid 'not much attention' or 'none at all', or had 'no idea' about the arrangements for their retirement incomes. The poll found that only 15 per cent of people paid 'a lot of attention' to their superannuation arrangements. This is astounding, even for young people, given how important retirement incomes are for people who are living longer and want a better standard of living in retirement.

Paradoxically, most people show little or no interest in their own finances, yet cost of living pressures dominate their concerns.

An odd thing about this lack of interest in personal finances is the high profile accorded to cost of living pressures in the general community, particularly among older people. Paradoxically, most people show little or no interest in their own finances, yet cost of living pressures dominate their concerns.

This financial complacency sees people with superannuation savings not bothering to check the details of how their money is being invested or the fees they are being charged, yet they lament loudly when at age 50, 55 or even 60 they realise they will not have enough savings to fund a decent retirement.

The Australian Taxation Office offers the startling statistic that there are 4 million unclaimed superannuation accounts, holding $18 billion in total assets. This is an extraordinary illustration of the lack of knowledge and interest so many have in their own financial fortunes. It is hard to fathom why people would not bother to keep track of or chase up their own money. Laziness? Too rich to worry? Or is it that they don't understand how superannuation works and how easily they can track their wealth accumulation and retirement income, along with their ability to add to it throughout their working life even when they change jobs.

A simple lack of effort to understand superannuation seems to be the most likely cause of this financial neglect. It could also be that many have built up a reliance on the government to 'fix things' when needed. In the case of retirement income, why should I bother if I spend all my money now and don't save for retirement, when I know there is a decent age pension to fall back on?

Government economic policy and personal finances are about money, wealth, wellbeing and comfort. Without money it is hard, if not impossible, to access a good education, good health care, a comfortable retirement—even, in more extreme although all too common cases, decent food, clothing and shelter.

Included in the broad category of personal wellbeing, of course, are issues relating to our environment and how the planet can sustain the 7.1 billion people currently on it, let alone the 10 billion or so predicted by 2050. Money, finances and wealth matters are the focus of this book. But I hope readers will be persuaded to take greater responsibility for their vote to ensure our politicians do things right, even if it involves each of us paying a bit more tax or paying more out of our own pocket for services. Over the longer run, good economic policy and good economic outcomes mean higher incomes and wealth for the whole economy. These benefits accrue, in large part, to you and me and directly improve our personal financial position. If we elect duds to federal or state government, and if we don't take an interest in what economic policies are implemented, we run the risk of missing out on a decent lifestyle not only now but into our retirement. This takes time, certainly, but a little effort in thinking about your economy can help to deliver high financial returns.

Think of it this way. It is mandatory for our teenage children to spend hour after hour learning how to drive competently, yet there is no requirement—or even much interest, I might say—to teach them about money, saving, debt, income and opportunity cost. Many people under the age of 25 have little or no idea about how to manage their money. Financial ignorance and a general indifference to money matters persist for most people throughout their lives. This helps to explain why, despite almost 25 years of strong economic growth in Australia, too many people still fall on economic hard times. Most people turn out to be good or excellent drivers as a result of the effort that went into teaching them. Most, unfortunately, have little clue about their finances or where all their money goes each week and wonder why they are unable to save enough for a comfortable retirement.

Financial ignorance and a general indifference to money matters persist for most people throughout their lives.

The reasons for this neglect of financial wellbeing are not entirely clear, given that the issues and coping techniques are relatively straightforward. Again, it is a bit like driving a car. Learning how to drive involves learning to pay attention, to watch out for the dangers and risks ahead. You learn the rules about what is safe so you don't speed; you don't drink and drive; and you maintain your car. The good news is you can still drive wherever you want and go 110 kilometres an hour on the freeway. Not bad. Barring the outside chance of an accident, you will be much better off for having learned how to drive, which allows you not only to get from A to B, but to do so in the safest possible way. If you learn the ins and outs of finance and pay attention to the rules that surround savings, investment and spending, then, barring an accident, you are likely to achieve financial security. With financial knowledge, you are less likely to be ripped off or to end your working career without adequate savings. And you are more likely to take actions that save money, such as negotiating a lower interest rate on your mortgage or lower fees on your superannuation, both of which are money saved.

If you learn the ins and outs of finance and pay attention to the rules that surround savings, investment and spending, then, barring an accident, you are likely to achieve financial security.

Planning, preparation and enthusiasm—an analogy

In examining why so few people bother to take more than a cursory look at their finances, it is instructive to consider an illustration that might at first seem at an odd tangent from a discussion of economic policy, finances and financial planning.

In recent years television has produced a boom in wonderfully entertaining cooking shows. One is the Ten Network's *Masterchef*. In this show otherwise ordinary people with a lot of interest, and possibly a bit of talent, use their skills and knowledge to cook what are often weird and wonderful meals. They do this with direction and advice from some of the best chefs in the world.

Often the contestants do a remarkable job. Sometimes they match the finesse of Heston Blumenthal or the flair and creativity of Gary Mehigan. The contestants' sense of euphoria and accomplishment when they cook a great dish that the judges enjoy and rank highly is palpable. But more often than not these incredible highs are not realised; the wannabe chefs fail to cut the mustard and their dishes are judged to be merely so-so.

There is drama when the truffle-infused beetroot risotto is overcooked and gluggy, or when the duck breast turns out to be raw inside despite the crispy skin. Sometimes the contestants are too slow at 'plating up', forget to drizzle the jus or misjudge the seasoning of the quail compote. These mistakes cost them dearly when it comes to qualifying for the next round or gaining that all-important immunity pin. But the judges, the masterchefs themselves, are there to guide the contestants on what went wrong, making sure that the next time they step up to the hot plate, their earlier mistakes are not repeated.

We might apply the *Masterchef* principles regarding effort, teaching and learning, and even entertainment, to our own economics and finances. There are, or at least there should be, similarities between planning for and preparing a meal and planning and preparing a business plan or investment decision. We know that every day businesses fail despite the best efforts and endeavours of those involved. Business results will often fall well short of the principals' objectives and dreams. This is because the people running the businesses and making the investment decisions are not the equivalent of the TV masterchefs.

There are, or at least there should be, similarities between planning for and preparing a meal and planning and preparing a business plan or investment decision.

Despite the crushing dismay of the contestants who are sent to the elimination challenge, in the real world a dodgy apricot chicken dish really doesn't matter all that much. For those who get through to the next round there is always tomorrow night to attempt to cook that restaurant-quality meal. When contestants do cook the equivalent of a dog's breakfast and must leave the show, tears are shed, there is a convulsion of bitter disappointment, but invariably they go home vowing to learn from their experience. Many go on to start a restaurant, café or catering business, using their newfound experience to embark on a new career. And the families of the *Masterchef* contestants will enjoy many culinary treats in the weeks and months after their loved ones leave the show and try out their new skills in the kitchen at home.

A model worth applying?

Of course, failures among *Masterchef* contestants have never triggered a recession or driven unemployment higher, nor have they increased economic inequality through a poor decision on tax reform or regulation of financial service advice. None of these culinary deficits have ruined the environment at a great cost to future generations. No one who forgot to plate up the port wine jus has lost their life savings as a result or been financially crippled by one of the few dodgy financial planners around the country. Nor have they implemented policies that trigger mass job losses or an inflationary spiral. Saucepan errors are only about fancy food not turning out to be fancy after all. Nothing more serious than that.

Which begs the question: why is there not a show called 'Master Economist'? Or 'Master Financial Planner'?

Let me make the case.

Contestants on such a show, and a few million viewers who might watch it, would soon become engrossed, I reckon, in seeing how their economy and the financial markets work. Imagine, they could be treated to a heated discussion between Westpac's Chief Economist, Bill Evans, ANZ's Warren Hogan and BT's Chris Caton on the commodity supercycle. Or they could watch and learn from AMP's Shane Oliver, NAB's Alan Oster and Commonwealth Bank's Michael Blythe as they discuss why the global growth cycle and commodity price swings will matter for the Australian economy. Think about it. They could see Mark Bouris, Alan Kohler and Marcus Padley go head to head on superannuation investment strategies and the benefits and pitfalls of investing in property, stocks, bonds or international markets.

How exciting would that be?

Imagine a masterclass with ex-Treasury and Reserve Bank of Australia officials such as Ken Henry, Bernie Fraser, Martin Parkinson or Ian Macfarlane talking about how they pulled the policy levers to reform our economy or how they reacted during the global financial crisis to make sure Australia did not fall into recession. What about having Gina Rinehart, Gail Kelly, John Symonds, James Packer or Frank Lowy talking about their business successes and how they did it? What a winner!

The prospects for this show are getting better and better.

But there's more. Let's throw in a few academic economists to round it out. Steve Keen could go on about the debt crisis and why we all will eventually be ruined because of debt. Warwick McKibbin could give some insights into the workings of the RBA, Australia's central bank, citing his experience on the board and action on climate change, while John Quiggin could reveal his thoughts on income distribution and wealth, and why inequality is a severe handbrake on economic growth. Let's also see what Bob Gregory has to say about the labour market and why Australia cannot enjoy a 3 per cent unemployment rate with current policy settings. What about ex-Treasurers Paul Keating, Peter Costello, Wayne Swan and John Howard going head to head? The likes of Professor Judith Sloan, Gerard Henderson, Chris Kenny and Terry McCrann could offer their whacky ideas on economic policy in a lighthearted 'bloopers and zingers' section.

The list of possible talent for the show is a mile long.

If this is not potentially as entertaining as the pressure test cook-off on a wagyu beef and pickled pear tartlet, I don't know what is. Participants and viewers could get to see world-class economists, policy leaders and financial experts discussing and debating the things that matter to every viewer's financial wellbeing. And they would all come away from such a show knowing the trade-offs in the policies our politicians need to implement for economic growth, jobs, wealth and financial fairness to be delivered.

Viewers could see the trade-offs involved when government policy is set.

Viewers would no doubt get to understand why economists, or at least some of us, are delighted with a strong retail sales report or are dismayed when the government fails to implement a policy change on taxation — for example, where the long-run benefits to the economy are obvious, but the political risks are considered to be too high. Viewers could see the trade-offs involved when government policy is set. Instead of wondering whether the lobster is overcooked, the master economists and contestants could work out what it might mean for Australia and our individual finances if the economic policymakers overcook the economy so inflation runs higher for several years, or if the RBA fails to cut interest rates when growth is too weak so the unemployment rate moves higher.

On a more personal level, viewers could see the risks and trade-offs involved when they choose to invest their superannuation in a balanced fund or a hedge fund or property or fixed income or an international growth option. Similarly, they could get a feel for what might lie ahead for their business as, for example, Australia's terms of trade fall away rapidly over the next few years as the world faces a glut of supply in the commodities that Australia produces. The show could have a 'forecasting and market predictions' section, which would be interesting in itself but would also help to sort out who the true master forecasters were.

In much the same way that we marvel at the ability of some *Masterchef* contestants as they reveal a near-perfect croquembouche, watching 'Master Economist' would give viewers insights into why the federal budget matters, why it is important that they think about their own business plan, superannuation, mortgage and personal finances as they move through life. It might even make some of them want to investigate whether any of that $18 billion in unclaimed superannuation money is theirs.

We might present a special challenge for our 'Master Economist' contestants: How do you deal with a budget deficit? What has led to the deficit? Which taxes should be hiked and which areas of government spending cut if we are to move back to a budget surplus? What are the consequences of raising the goods and services tax, for example, and how could the extra revenue for the government from such a tax hike alter the nation's finances? What to do about government spending cuts? Defence is an easy option to cut, especially considering those expensive submarines being built in South Australia ... or is it? What are the implications of making such a cut? What would it mean if the 'Master Economist' contestant advocated a cut in spending on education? Sure, it might see the budget move to surplus in the next few years, but what about over the longer term when Australia is left with a poorly educated, low-skilled workforce?

I could go on!

These are the sorts of questions policymakers in government confront every day. Little wonder it is a tough job, or that when a decision is made some sectors of the community will feel hard done by — and will voice their views — while others will delight in the government's largesse.

Answers from contestants could be monitored by the policy experts, who would no doubt impart their own wisdom, including pointing out that most policy changes have consequences elsewhere in the economy and that different sections of the economy win or lose when policies are changed. A simplistic case in point is lifting the GST rate to help move the budget back to surplus.

ECONOMICS AS NEWS

An example of the lack of interest in economics and coverage of economic news arose as I was writing this book. In October 2014 it was reported that consumer sentiment remained very weak. Consumers were pessimistic because their wages were falling in real terms, employment prospects were deteriorating as the unemployment rate moved higher, and some stock market ructions were unfolding that threatened household wealth—all of which contributed to making consumers a bit cautious about the future. The weak consumer sentiment helped to explain why growth in housing consumption spending was subdued, which was holding back the overall pace of economic growth.

But just as this important economic information was being released, out came the news that Parramatta footballer Jarryd Hayne was leaving rugby league to play gridiron in the US. Good on him, of course, but so what?

The news for the next 24 hours was dominated by Hayne's move. Is he big enough, fast enough? Which team will he play for? All these known unknowns that e-journalists make up to pad out a shallow story. The economic news on consumer sentiment, and what it meant for interest rates, your business, your superannuation and the economy more generally, barely got further mention.

I know what news item was of greater importance that day—not that many people heard about it!

The importance of engagement

It shouldn't be that difficult to find a place for economics and finance in the popular mindset and to have the media report it as enthusiastically and insightfully as they cover a sports star's planned move overseas. The trade-offs, intended and unintended consequences, and even the more obscure effects of policy changes, are material for heated and worthwhile discussions. It is often a philosophical choice for a government to decide where to make spending cuts and hike taxes as they manage their budget. Some governments opt to save money through cuts to education funding, which may be good for the budget in the short term but will mean a longer run cost to the economy as the skill level of the workforce falls. Strangely, this is a choice some inept politicians willingly make.

Other governments have a long-term strategy and will put a price on carbon emissions so that non-carbon emitting sources of energy can be established, flourish and eventually replace carbon-producing sources. The price on carbon was also designed to make you and me, households and businesses, cut back our use of energy with a view to addressing the current trend of climate change, which may well cripple the global economy in the decades ahead.

Despite all of the potential benefits from learning about the economy, investing and policymaking, in reality it is all but impossible to imagine a television show called 'Master Economist' getting off the ground. I would forecast that prospective audience numbers would be much too low. Not many would want to hear, for example, that having a gap year after school but before university will cost you somewhere around $50 000 — so don't do it! Or that you will have to pay more tax or have some other government benefit eliminated if you want good health care for your family, good aged care for your parents, good education standards for your kids, good roads to drive on and the nation defended securely.

This is not a message that many people will readily tune in to, even though they should. What's more, few will like to be told, you spend five times more on takeaway food, beer and wine than you do on electricity, so stop spending up on that Pad Thai and cheeky Sauvignon Blanc so you don't have to worry too much when the next electricity bill comes in. You will have more than enough to cover the bill when it comes in if you eat at home a bit more often.

I want to see people more engaged with their finances, with a firmer grasp of their financial wellbeing and a better understanding and awareness of the choices and trade-offs. As you read this book you need to be aware of some basic economic facts relating to the size of the Australian economy and how vitally important good policy, good business decisions and sound investment strategies are if our economic position is to be sustained for the next few years.

I want to see people more engaged with their finances, with a firmer grasp of their financial wellbeing and a better understanding and awareness of the choices and trade-offs.

For example, superannuation assets have a value of just under $2.0 trillion, according to ABS data. The value of housing Australians own to live in and for investment is around $5.5 trillion. Household debt is around $1.25 trillion. By the way, $1 trillion is $1 000 000 000 000.00, or about the average annual wage of 1.25 million workers. These numbers are big and illustrate how marginal changes in the economy or in markets can yield significant financial changes.

How much of the $2.0 trillion in superannuation is yours? Where is that money invested? Stocks? Term deposits? Property? Bonds? Have you borrowed money in your superannuation fund to buy a property? What about that huge sum of money in housing assets and that mortgage debt? Is it a problem for the Australian economy that house prices are high and mortgage borrowings are so large, or is it a sign of confidence that prudent borrowers are borrowing and lenders are lending and, as a result, the economy grows?

The economy, interest rates, economic policy choices and your decisions on your finances, for example, all impact directly on these superannuation savings, and on managing that debt and minimising the inevitable risks associated with matters economic and financial. It is well nigh impossible to forecast recessions, global booms or busts, market gyrations or some of the huge but inevitable structural changes in the global economy, but these things happen frequently and they matter to you. Being aware of the risks as these trends unfold is better than having your head in the sand or, worse, not knowing what to do when these shocks loom.

Economics and finance, whether at the personal, business or government level, are not that complex. Or rather, they do not need to be that complex. Most issues can be boiled down to practical, real-world applications that with a bit of care and work can help you manage your financial position from a position of knowledge and strength. These range from knowing why it matters if there is a rise in the Chinese yuan or a fall in the Dow Jones Industrial Average, or what the latest interest rate change from the RBA means for you and, equally significant, why it was made.

Most issues can be boiled down to practical, real-world applications that with a bit of care and work can help you manage your financial position from a position of knowledge and strength.

These decisions are vitally important to you and me, as are changes to our tax system and structural changes that occur within the economy as the technology revolution continues. Why is a carbon tax bad and the goods and services tax good, according to the recent political mantra? Why is it bad that manufacturing in Australia is declining when services are growing so strongly? Why do some see a budget surplus as good and a deficit as bad? Which really matters when it comes to the economy?

It is not all that hard to get a decent understanding of the drivers of your business, your personal finances and the strategies you need to adopt to deal with inevitable changes in economic and financial circumstances from month to month or year to year. That doesn't mean you will be able to avoid every unpleasant event that unfolds. Nor does it mean that you won't have to swallow some unpleasant medicine to help fix financial problems or to start building your financial position for the future. And nor will it mean that every decision you make will be the right one. There are too many unknowns. Everyone now knows smoking is bad for your health and since people were made aware of and accepted this unpleasant fact, smoking levels have plummeted. Yet very few people who are saving, investing, borrowing and working know—or are willing to accept—that spending too much at the wrong time is bad for your long-term financial health, just as more borrowing and debt and investment may be desirable when the time is right.

Why do some see a budget surplus as good and a deficit as bad? Which really matters when it comes to the economy?

This book takes a baby step or two towards addressing the current gap in financial understanding, helping readers to appreciate economic news and be better equipped to critique the big-picture policy issues. By working out why the economy and economic news matter to you and to everyone, and being prepared to understand the challenges of running a business and your personal finances, you will surely make better decisions that will help rather than hinder your long-run financial security.

KEY POINTS

- Be aware of what is happening in the broader economy.
- Know what economic policies are likely to change and think on their possible impact on you.
- Keep an open mind. Economies and the market change every day — does your business strategy or investment plan change as well?
- Pay attention to the economic news — it matters.
- Don't just talk to your children about money — teach them how to manage it.

chapter two
YOUR ECONOMY

Morning, noon and night, every TV news channel, most radio networks and countless online websites give financial market updates. It is like a race call on changes in the stock market or the Australian dollar. There may be a fleeting mention of some economic data, then the oil and gold price are updated. If the RBA has changed interest rates, there is usually a comment about what it means for the average mortgage, along the lines of 'this interest rate rise will cost the average mortgage holder an extra $40 a month' or some such sound grab.

This is all useful information. But rarely is there any effort to drill down into why interest rates were raised, why the stock market fell or what may be the consequences for the economy and your savings from such a movement. Or indeed when there is a change in oil prices or a certain stock. Oddly, these finance reports never mention bond markets, which deal in the yield or interest rate earned by investors on the money borrowed by governments around the world, including here in Australia. At times of economic crisis, the 'safe-haven' of government bonds sees yields fall sharply, and when there is a country-specific disaster, such as the threat of Russia or Greece defaulting on their debt, the interest rate skyrockets. It should be noted that the market for government bonds is larger and has greater turnover than the stock market and has proven to offer a better gauge of economic and market risks than share prices.

The brevity of these media market grabs precludes a more detailed coverage. Nevertheless it is important to know why markets and the economy are changing. Let's look at how the economy, markets and some of these policy issues work and what changes in these can mean.

Economic literacy—understanding the linkages

Higher interest rates are almost inevitably associated with a strong economy. A strong economy generally leads to capacity constraints and rising inflation pressures. These, in turn, mean that the interest rate rises are likely to coincide with a strong stock market and gains in the average household's superannuation nest egg. I don't think I have ever noticed that mentioned in a TV market report when the Australian Stock Exchange (ASX) has risen, say, 1 or 2 per cent in a day.

For the Australian economy, and therefore for Australians, low petrol prices are bad news.

It is the same with the inevitable media beat-up when petrol prices fall. When there are global market ructions, the oil price drops and that translates into, say, a five cents a litre fall in the Australian petrol price, we seem to get very excited about how beneficial it is for the 'family budget'. This 5 cents a litre drop translates into a saving of around $3.50 a tank, which as we know is about the price of a single latte at any decent coffee shop. It is, in other words, chickenfeed and blown out of all proportion.

Not that this is reported, but for the Australian economy, and therefore for Australians, low petrol prices are bad news. Australia is a net exporter of energy and when oil prices fall, there is usually an accompanying fall in the price of other energy resources, such as natural gas and coal. Other commodity prices are usually weaker too. As these prices fall, the Australian economy is likely to become weaker, the national income lower and the share price of those energy-producing companies also pushed lower.

You will no doubt cheer that $3.50 saving you make as you fill up the car, but it would be safe to say that the lower oil price has undermined the performance of the economy and taken away more than $3.50 from the value of your superannuation assets given they are likely to include some money invested in the local oil, coal and gas companies, as well as the big resources stocks.

FALLING PETROL PRICES ARE BAD NEWS FOR YOU

The following article is from my blog at thekouk.com in December 2014, when the global oil price was falling sharply.

Falling oil prices are poison for the Australian economy. That hasn't stopped the perpetual optimists noting that at current levels, the oil price fall will translate to falling petrol prices and a saving of around $20 a month in the average household's petrol spending. Happy days!

What they fail to mention is that the oil price fall coincides directly with collapsing prices for other energy resources — notably coal and gas. So while the average motorist will save $20 a month on their petrol purchases, their superannuation fund will have been smashed as the share price of stocks in this space react to the increasingly dismal profit outlook.

So save $20 a month on petrol — great. Drop in wealth — worse by a large margin.

Oh, there is also the point that weak commodity prices hurt Australian national income, economic growth and by definition employment. Hope those losing out as share prices fall and job prospects deteriorate rejoice when they save 15 to 20 cents a litre on their petrol purchase. It is a trade-off where Australia loses out. Big time.

It is these sorts of linkages that make the economy, economic policy and financial markets so interesting, so important and worthy of much more attention, especially for people whose lives are inexorably tied up in each of these bits of economic and financial news. Impacted too is the superficial and misplaced euphoria seen when the petrol price goes down a couple of cents.

In terms of the big-picture view of the economy, Australia's total economic output in 2015 will be approximately $1.7 trillion and this is set to rise to close to $2 trillion by 2020. Every day, the collective efforts of 24 million Australians will produce about $5 billion worth of goods and services. That is $5 billion every day, weekends and public holidays included. Most of the time we probably don't even know we are generating this huge amount of economic activity. We create this income — or gross domestic product (GDP) — as we go about our lives, buying food, insuring the car, exporting iron ore, going to the movies, staying in a hotel, preparing a restaurant meal for a tourist from China, building a road, preparing a tax return, driving a truck, laying bricks, acting in a play, growing a lettuce, writing a book, seeing the doctor, buying a computer or having a green tea at our favourite coffee shop. All these activities contribute to GDP.

Indeed, it is the aggregate of these activities that make up the Australian economy.

Every day, the collective efforts of 24 million Australians will produce about $5 billion worth of goods and services.

There are over eleven and a half million people in paid work in Australia doing their bit to produce these goods and services. If the economy continues to grow at a decent rate, which is the critical issue underpinning the chapters ahead in this book, there will be 12 million people in a job by 2018.

We need policymakers to do all they can to maintain this economic and employment growth in a sustainable way. Business needs to show flair and entrepreneurship unconstrained by poor or restrictive government policies. Consumers need to save a bit, spend a bit and borrow a bit, according to their life cycle and financial circumstances. The wealthier people are and the higher their wages and incomes, the more they can spend to help sustain the economy.

These numbers are impressive. Put in context, they show how wonderful the opportunities are for business in Australia. It has been 24 years since the last recession. This makes Australia a global standout.

The numbers for Australia also suggest there are some attendant risks in such a large economy. Twenty-four years without a recession is unprecedented in Australia. On a simple balance of probability assessment, we are due for one. After such a run, a big economy such as Australia's has many soft points that a change in luck or a policy error could expose, hurting economic growth and leading to severe economic weakness.

Will it be a result of a collapse in commodity prices, a fall in house prices, a mistake by the government in cutting spending as it strives for a budget surplus, or will it be triggered by the RBA holding monetary policy too tight for too long? We cannot be sure.

It is fascinating to note that according to World Bank data Australia is now the twelfth largest economy in the world, making up 2.1 per cent of world GDP. This is a potent statistic, especially since Australia makes up only 0.3 per cent of the world's population.

These simple facts show just how dramatically Australia punches above its weight in economic terms and why the Aussie dollar and the stock and bond markets are such a critical investment allocation for fund managers around the world. At present, Australia is a great place to invest.

Twenty-four years without a recession is unprecedented in Australia. On a simple balance of probability assessment, we are due for one.

But it is not just the big global investors who can see opportunities in Australia as they continue to invest heavily in our stock, bond and property markets.

The size and power of the Australian economy over the past generation highlight the strength and opportunities that Australia offers for big and small business and for all Australians. Being part of an economy that is growing, with a dynamic, skilled and educated population and with low unemployment, and is located close to Asia (the fastest growing economic region of the world), is obviously good news. It should go without saying that having a strong economy is superior to having one that is floundering with weak growth, failing social structures and limited prospects for a return to strong and sustained growth.

In other words, would you prefer to have had your investment money in an economy like Australia with sustained economic growth, generally low inflation and government debt that is rated triple-A or in Spain, for example, which is mired in recession with chronically high unemployment and government debt flirting with junk status?

While the examples are not strictly comparable, would you prefer to invest your money in a company that grows each year and has low levels of debt or one that is hugely volatile, has recently been going backwards and has a debt level that it has trouble servicing? The answer should be very straightforward.

The data show that our individual wealth and financial wellbeing have never been higher. According to the International Monetary Fund, Australia's per capita GDP in US dollar terms is fifth, behind only Luxembourg, Norway, Qatar and Switzerland. On this basis, per capita GDP in Australia is over 20 per cent higher than that of the US and Canada; it is nearly 50 per cent above that of Germany, France and New Zealand and is roughly double that of Italy and Spain.

On purchasing power parity, which takes account of the relative cost of living in each country, Australian per capita GDP is tenth, with the likes of Singapore, Brunei, the US, San Marino and Canada having a slightly higher income. Australians' incomes and standard of living, on this measure, are still massively above those of the bulk of the seemingly well-off countries in Europe and Asia.

Whichever way you cut it, the dynamics of the Australian economy and its population are impressive. We are rich. It explains why Australian wages are among the highest in the world and why house prices are so very high not only in the main cities, but also in regional towns.

In other words, people in low-income countries with low per capita GDP have low wages, low house prices and, with that, poorer standards of living. Think of this and you can see why houses in Sydney, London, New York or Toronto are expensive while in Syria, Iraq and Southern Sudan they are cheap.

In Australia's case, wealth and prosperity do not filter down equally to every individual or business. Some people and sectors do better than others. This is where the role of government is important — in spreading the benefits of unprecedented wealth via universal access to health care, education, decent levels of income and other socially progressive policies.

In Australia's case, wealth and prosperity do not filter down equally to every individual or business. Some people and sectors do better than others. This is where the role of government is important.

From a big-picture macroeconomic point of view a future economic downturn, including the possibility of a recession, could see these impressive dynamics reverse. There is always the risk that a change in economic luck, a global economic shock, or poor economic policy choices by the government or the RBA could see the economy turn lower.

With what looks to be an unfolding long-run decline in commodity prices and Australia's terms of trade (see figure 2.1, overleaf), there is a strong probability that the next 5 to 10 years will be a lot tougher than the past 10, with income growth slower. The terms of trade measure the price of the goods and services Australia exports (iron ore, coal, tourism, education, gold and the like) divided by the price of the goods and services Australia imports (cars, computers, clothes, machinery and the like). The higher the price for our exports and the lower the price we pay for our imports, the higher the terms of trade — and, as we are witnessing now, vice versa.

This decline in the terms of trade, dare I say it, increases the risk of a long-overdue recession.

These and a range of other macroeconomic changes, combined with swings in commodity prices and the Aussie dollar, the government budget and moves in global financial markets, inevitably will impact on key parts of your business, your family, your house and your retirement.

Figure 2.1: Australia's terms of trade over time

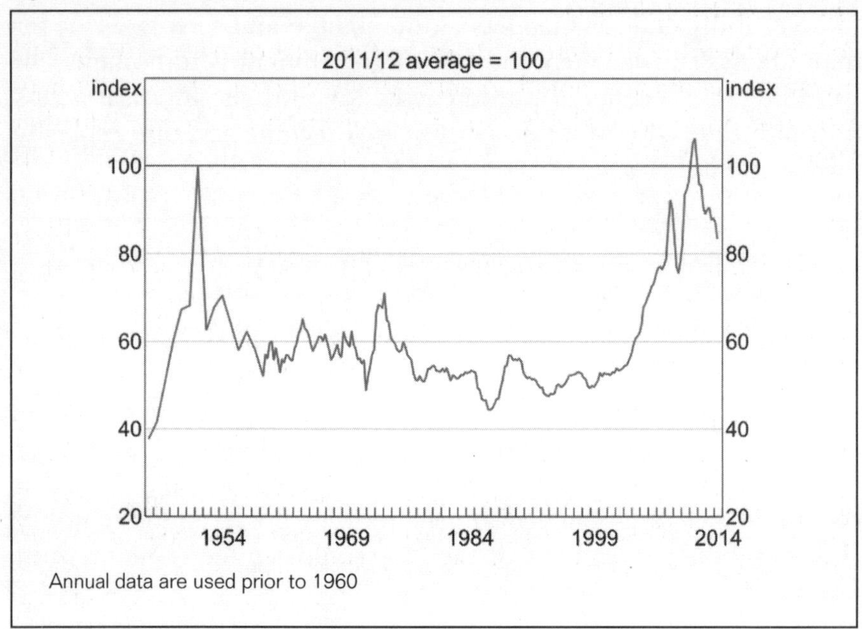

Source: © Australian Bureau of Statistics 2015; © Reserve Bank of Australia 2001–2015.

I will outline some pivotal issues to be aware of as you plan for each stage of your life, looking at factors that will almost inevitably impact on your finances. I will also flag some of the uncertainties lurking beneath the surface that just might emerge to create opportunities to be embraced or pitfalls to be avoided.

Dynamics within the Australian economy are what drive good economists to care about the monthly data flow on business conditions, the number of new houses to be built, credit growth, employment, inflation, exports, house prices, the stock market, bond yields and business investment, to name just a few factors. These economic indicators matter not only specifically for the operation of a business and personal finances. Large macroeconomic and financial market swings will force the RBA to adjust interest rates, impacting on every borrower and saver, and they will drive the Australian dollar well away from where it might have been when you set your business plan. If the shocks are large enough, they will also force the government to adjust its policies on tax, spending and borrowing.

Interest rates

To state the obvious, interest rates matter for borrowers, savers and investors. As already noted, Australians have over $1.25 trillion in mortgage and personal debt while the business sector has a further $900 billion of borrowings from banks. At 6 per cent, the interest bill for business and householders is around $130 billion a year. A one percentage point shift in interest rates means more than a $20 billion swing in annual interest costs or savings for the indebted sectors of the economy. Twenty billion dollars with just one percentage point! No wonder the RBA is so cautious about adjusting interest rate settings and nowadays usually moves rates in increments of a quarter of a percentage point.

A one percentage point shift in interest rates means more than a $20 billion swing in annual interest costs or savings for the indebted sectors of the economy.

This is why those of you with debt need to have a good feel for interest rate risks over the long run—say, the life of a 10-, 15- or 20-year mortgage—as well as your floating or variable business loan and overdraft. Next month's possible interest rate change of 0.25 per cent may seem important when it happens, but over the longer term it will almost certainly be small beer among many interest rate changes that will see rates revert to a longer run average, perhaps some two, three or four percentage points higher than today. And this is when the consequences will be huge for your cash flow and how you manage your debt.

Although there is little to be gained from interest rate paranoia—that is, obsessing with each actual or expected tweak in monetary policy from the RBA—borrowers should always keep in the back of their mind the idea that interest rates can and at some stage will go up, even if none of the market 'experts' are predicting it. They may be wrong, and all you are doing by looking at interest rate risks is scenario planning. It is prudent to be cautious when working out how much extra per month you will need to find if interest rates rise, say, two percentage points from where they are today. Can you cope with this hit to your cash flow? If so, terrific. If not, you had better start to think of ways to reduce your debt levels or improve cash flows from elsewhere, because that risk of higher interest rates will always be there.

SOME MORTGAGE INTEREST RATE FACTS

Australia's mortgage interest rate history should be known to everyone with debt.

Let's go back over the past quarter century or so to review some of the extremes that have been reached.

In 1989 and 1990 the standard variable interest rate reached 17 per cent. Here is a fun thing to do: put that number into your mortgage calculator and watch it explode. Mortgage rates in 2015, at around 5.5 per cent, are the lowest ever recorded in Australia. By way of illustration, the monthly repayments on a 25-year $300 000 mortgage with interest rates at 5.5 per cent are around $1842 a month or just over $22 000 a year. A 17 per cent mortgage rate increases the monthly repayments to $4313 per month or almost $52 000 a year.

No one is suggesting interest rates will reach 17 per cent again, but even if you plug a 9.6 per cent interest rate into the calculator, monthly repayments rise to $2642, or $31 700 a year—almost $10 000 more than on current interest rates.

Why 9.6 per cent? For those who have forgotten, that was the mortgage rate in 2008, just seven years ago.

Without overemphasising the significance of peaks and troughs in the interest rate cycle, examining some long-run averages offers a good guide to where your mortgage interest rate might gravitate to over the course of your loan. Over the past 10 years, the standard mortgage interest rate has averaged 7.2 per cent—well above where it is in 2015 (see figure 2.2). Over the past 20 years, the standard mortgage rate has averaged around 7.4 per cent, remarkably similar to the 10-year average.

This is reassuring. It is safe to say (and prudent to plan accordingly) that over the next 10 years your mortgage interest rate will average in the low 7 per cent region, rather than the low to mid 5 per cent levels we have become used to in the past couple of years.

Figure 2.2: Australian mortgage lending rates

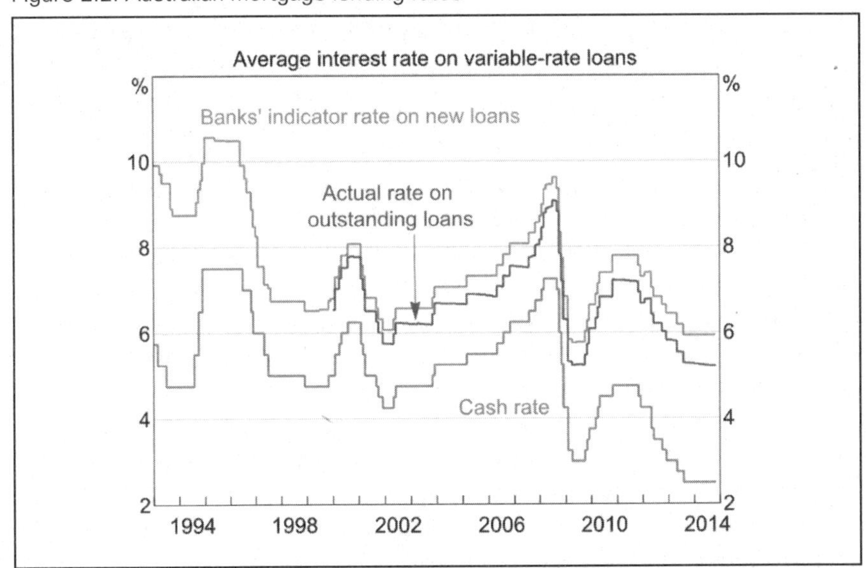

Source: Australian Bureau of Statistics 2015; © Australian Prudential Regulation Authority 2015; © Perpetual Limited 2015; © Reserve Bank of Australia 2001–2014.

Once you have made allowance for the possibility of higher interest rates, the good news in terms of your borrowing costs would be that they do not eventuate. In these circumstances, you would clearly have either a bigger buffer for future interest rate rises or some spare cash with which you could pay off some more of your loan—not bad outcomes from some prudent contingency planning.

The older you get, the more important term deposits and the associated level of interest rates become.

Interest rates also have significant implications for savers, especially those in retirement, those looking to accumulate a deposit to buy a house or investors who rely on the relative safety of term deposits for a steady income flow. Unlike young people who can weather a few market ructions in their superannuation fund over the course of a couple of decades, many retirees with superannuation investments simply do not have the benefit of time to see their wealth recover when risky investments slide, as they do from time to time. The older you get, the more important term deposits and the associated level of interest rates become. I will touch on this further in chapter 5.

The economy is critically important for investment returns, whether in property, stocks, bonds or term deposits. The fallout from the stock market free-fall in the period from 2008 to 2010 is a classic case in which many retirees, lured by what had been a stunningly powerful surge in stocks in the four or five years previously, neglected the risk management aspect of their finances. Many did not plan for the possibility of a fall in share prices and as a result remained heavily invested in stocks with very little in the way of government bonds or term deposits when the global crisis hit. As the global economy cascaded into recession, stock prices throughout the world including Australia fell around 50 per cent. This severely damaged the retirement plans of many. Those caught up in this economic and market upheaval who thought they were set for a comfortable retirement were left dreadfully short. And this, I note in passing, was when term deposits were yielding a solid 6 or 7 per cent.

The economy is critically important for investment returns, whether in property, stocks, bonds or term deposits.

As for interest rates, the levels of private sector debt and household savings are reasons why the monthly RBA Board meeting gets so much attention in the media and the financial markets. Will it cut or raise interest rates? The answer to that question matters for most people, either as individuals with mortgage and personal debt, savings and investments or in their business capacity with a loan or overdraft. The RBA decision on interest rates, quite plainly, depends on its reading of current economic conditions and judgement of the outlook, especially for inflation.

Despite the hype surrounding the RBA and its announcements, the fact is that around three-quarters of its monthly meetings end with a decision to leave the official interest rates unchanged. Mostly, all that fuss is about nothing. But when the RBA does decide that interest rates need to swing, it often opts for two, three or even four interest rate adjustments over a five- or six-month period. Someone (I am not sure who came up with the phrase first) made the nice point that interest rate adjustments from the RBA are a bit like cockroaches—there is never just one; when they happen there are always two or more.

Given the RBA has an explicit target to keep inflation at between 2 and 3 per cent over the course of the business cycle, if economic pressures see inflation moving outside this band, it will usually set higher interest rates with high inflation and lower interest rates with low inflation. It does this with a view to growing the economy at a strong yet sustainable pace. This inflation target is a critical reason why the RBA frequently starts adjusting interest rates in the month after a quarterly inflation figure is released. The news on inflation often requires an interest rate response if the integrity of the inflation target is to be maintained.

Going for growth—the role of surplus or deficit

A critical issue often overlooked in the contemporary economic debate is that economic growth is good. Without it, jobs and incomes stagnate or even fall. To have the financial resources to meet the ever-increasing demand for high-quality health and aged care facilities, to have more efficient infrastructure, including better roads, schools, university and training facilities—all need a strongly growing economy to provide the capacity to fund these measures either through the private sector or via the government.

Economic growth is good. Without it, jobs and incomes stagnate or even fall.

One only has to review the catastrophic situation in the US and throughout Europe during and since the 2008 global financial crisis when the deep recession unfolded. Governments were running massive budget deficits as they collected little tax while funding massively expensive bank rescues and other bailouts of the private sector. These cash-strapped governments had little or no capacity to meet the demands of society for health, education and infrastructure because they and the private sector did not have the financial wherewithal to undertake these services. So services were heavily cut as struggling governments tried to limit the extent of the budget deficit blowout. In a recession, in addition to the obvious hit to living standards of the unemployed and those suffering wage cuts, improved access to health care, new infrastructure programs and the like are also curtailed.

This is why, when it comes to managing an economy, good economists and policymakers will do everything possible to avoid a recession. This includes using policy options such as cutting interest rates, letting the currency (the Australian dollar) fall, introducing quantitative easing, and using fiscal policy to boost government spending and lower the tax take from the private sector. All of these policies add to GDP growth and the pace of job creation.

WHAT IS A GOOD ECONOMY?

What is good economic management?

Unfortunately, the determination of what makes a 'good economic manager' has been clouded in recent years by what has often been misinformed dogma on what good economic policy is all about.

Let's start at the end.

At a macroeconomic level, if policymakers in Australia can deliver annual GDP growth of 3 per cent, inflation between 2 and 3 per cent, and an unemployment rate at 4 or 5 point something, and preside over rising living standards, that will be as good as it gets. For all credible economists, this is the unquestioned, universally agreed end game for national policymakers.

The budget surplus or deficit, level of debt, interest rates and value of the Australian dollar are the tools used to achieve these objectives. They are not, in themselves, the target.

This is often overlooked in the misrepresentation of low interest rates as good, government debt as bad and the deficit as a sign of mismanagement. Many people mistakenly think these factors should be the target rather than levers to be pulled by policymakers.

Think about it. What good would a budget surplus be if the economy were in recession and the unemployment rate were 8 or 10 per cent? What good are low interest rates if 5 per cent inflation is eating away at consumer purchasing power and Australia's international competitiveness?

No good!

Or, perhaps viewed the way it should be, how good is it when policymakers run a temporary budget deficit to keep the unemployment rate below 6 per cent or when high interest rates cool the economy to lock in low inflation?

Very good!

It comes back to the point I often make. Any monkey with an Excel spreadsheet can deliver a budget surplus. Cut government programs and spending and hike taxes and there you have it — the budget is in surplus.

This simple approach is worse than unhelpful — indeed it is positively damaging — as it takes no account of the position of the business cycle.

A budget deficit is like a cold and rainy day. Is a cold, rainy day good or bad? If you are holidaymaker at the beach then clearly it is disappointing. But if you are a farmer on land that has not received much rain over the past two years, then the rain will be very welcome.

So too with a budget deficit. In a booming economy, a deficit is inappropriate, but in a period of weak growth it is highly desirable, even necessary.

This is why political point scoring around delivering lower interest rates or a surplus are misguided and dangerous.

Crucially, it is what happens to GDP, inflation and unemployment that largely determines the appropriate level of interest rates, the state of the budget and whether or not the economy has been well managed.

What's more, bad luck can get in the way of the best policy settings. A global recession, an overvalued Australian dollar or a natural disaster can have consequences for policy bottom lines and for the real economy.

If the world is economically weak, interest rates will inevitably be lower and the budget more inclined to be in deficit. And that is the way it should be, because these policy reactions will help to insulate the local economy from the negative global developments. It would smack of policy incompetence, and reckless economic vandalism, if interest rates were allowed to remain high and the government cut spending and hiked taxes to ensure the budget stayed in surplus when the economy was weak.

In the recent budget debate in Australia there was much truth in the suggestion that programs covering such important matters as education, aged care and disability care cannot be funded or improved on if the budget is in permanent and large deficit. Some tax tweaks and spending moderation are needed elsewhere in the array of government taxing and spending powers if these and other programs are to be provided at a decent standard over many years. The economy also needs to continue to grow at a decent pace if employment levels are to be supported and the budget position of the government is to be held in decent shape.

This, in turn, leads to another vital economic issue—Australia's budgetary or fiscal position. There is no doubt that Australian government finances are among the best in the world. Government debt is incredibly low. The budget deficit is peanuts as a share of GDP and this reflects the fact that, with very few exceptions, public finances have been well managed for over four decades. There is no serious economist who would dispute the fact that the budget has been managed with aplomb. Over many decades, this has involved moving to a budget deficit when the economy has been weak or below its trend pace of GDP growth and then returning to surplus once the economy has sustained a period of above-trend growth and the unemployment rate has fallen to an acceptable level.

The budget deficit is peanuts as a share of GDP and this reflects the fact that, with very few exceptions, public finances have been well managed for over four decades.

This balancing of the budget over the economic cycle has seen government debt remain at extraordinarily low levels, even when there has been substantial fiscal policy stimulus at times of global recession. That said, Australia is now experiencing a more positive long-run economic cycle, which means that over the next few years there should be a gradual move towards getting the budget back to surplus. This will need a set of policies from the government that will inevitably impact on business conditions and your personal finances. A budget surplus means quite simply the government is taking more money out of the economy than it is putting in. If this is because the economy is booming, private sector spending is strong and tax receipts for the government are flooding in, the impact on the average hip pocket and business account will be moderate. If it occurs when there are pockets of economic weakness, or even if there is only a moderate economic expansion, the move to surplus would be more noticeable and likely more restrictive.

Whatever exigencies emerge, the likely strategy of government will be oriented to the proverbial saving for a raining day—building finances to a point that protects the economy against the day when the next global economic shock or recession threatens to hit our shores.

It seems unlikely that the government can simply rely on a robust pace of economic growth to get back to budget surplus. It won't happen by itself.

This is why the budget settings will be so important for the whole economy over the next few years. The critically important fiscal policy questions will be what taxes will be increased and where government spending will be cut. Both sides of politics know that with reasonable rates of economic growth, the return to a budget surplus is essential and desirable over time. It is how they get there that is the challenge, not only for the politicians, but also for the business sector and households. It seems unlikely that the government can simply rely on a robust pace of economic growth to get back to budget surplus. It won't happen by itself.

A more problematic scenario would be one in which the economy was weak, perhaps very weak, for an extended period of time. This would mean government revenue was further undermined by low company and income taxes, and expenditures increased. By definition, this would lead to larger and ongoing budget deficits, which in turn would require a complete overhaul of the policy priorities of the government of the day. The way the economy has entered 2015, this may well be an issue for the next year or two and will not doubt be a dominant issue for all political parties in the 2016 federal election.

Understanding these policy dynamics matters because, at the personal level, most of us either work for a wage, make and draw a profit from the business we run, live off our retirement savings or have a government income to support us in old age, education or when we occasionally fall on hard times. Changes to government policy can and will have an impact on our take-home incomes. Witness the recent history of tax cuts, pension increases and tax treatment of superannuation, to name a few areas.

Where you live and work

There are many other issues to consider when thinking about your economy. Within the Australian economy, there are substantial variations in the economic performance of different industry sectors and in different geographical areas. In recent years, there has been the common call of a multi-speed or patchwork economy, two terms that try to capture the themes of divergence, for example between manufacturing and mining, between Tasmania and Western Australia, and even between Sydney and Canberra.

Where people live and the sector in which they work can have a huge impact on their financial wellbeing, even if in a big-picture macroeconomic sense Australia is one of the standout countries of the world. Those exposed to the manufacturing sector in recent years have had it tough, while those in mining and housing construction have done well. But in economics there are cycles. We are now seeing the mining sector slump with investment and employment declining as commodity prices fall and supply of mining output from countries outside Australia increases. And now tourism and education are growing, in large part due to the lower Australian dollar and ongoing solid economic growth in the regions that attracts greater numbers of foreign tourists and students to our shores. The lower Australian dollar is also seeing something of a revival in manufacturing, albeit from a position a year or two ago of severe decline.

Those exposed to the manufacturing sector in recent years have had it tough, while those in mining and housing construction have done well. But in economics there are cycles.

The chronic structural weaknesses within the Tasmanian economy make it very difficult to see where its strong growth can come from. New South Wales recently has been expanding at a solid pace with growth in housing, banking, finance, accounting and legal industries.

The unemployment rate: what should we accept or expect?

One area that has been neglected in the economic debate in Australia is a target for the unemployment rate (see figure 2.3). Over the past few years, ongoing subdued national economic growth has seen the unemployment rate edge up from around 4.5 per cent to around 6.25 to 6.5 per cent. While this is not a recessionary-level disaster for the economy, no serious commentator or policymaker for that matter would be content to see the unemployment rate remain above 6 per cent over any long time frame. But should we be happy with even 5 per cent when 4 or 3 per cent might be achievable?

Figure 2.3: Australian unemployment rate, 1993–2014

Source: © Australian Bureau of Statistics 2015.

The business cycles over the past few decades suggest that politicians and policymakers are happy to claim 'full employment' when the unemployment rate is about 5 per cent. Anything less and skills shortages and wage pressures build and it is left to the RBA to hike interest rates to cool demand for workers.

It seems inequitable, unfair and frankly a policy copout to be content with, at best, one in 20 of the working-age population out of a job. And having the RBA hiking interest rates to implicitly discourage firms from hiring, as it did in 2007 and early 2008, indicates there are important shortcomings in Australia's policy priorities.

This is not to say the lack of a target for unemployment is the fault of the RBA. Rather, it is the structure of the labour market that means Australia has elevated inflation risks whenever the unemployment rate has fallen to around the 5 per cent level. At 5 per cent unemployment, skills shortages start to emerge, upside wage pressures start to build and the upper band of the RBA's 2 to 3 per cent target is put at risk.

The objective, therefore, is to lower the level of unemployment at which those wages and inflation pressures build.

When discussing the labour market, most politicians tend to focus on the number of jobs created rather than the unemployment rate. This is a weak approach given that population growth will deliver some 175 000 to 200 000 'new jobs' every year if the economy grows at about its trend pace.

Politicians who deliver a sound-grab promising to 'create one million new jobs over five years' are actually doing nothing at all to reduce the unemployment rate. They are merely suggesting they hope to see the economy grow at its long-rate trend pace and that jobs created match population growth and no more. Big deal! Big achievement!

Politicians who deliver a sound-grab promising to 'create one million new jobs over five years' are actually doing nothing at all to reduce the unemployment rate.

Australia has not had a target for the unemployment rate for many decades. This is probably because of the fear of failure among politicians and the often unpopular policies that would be needed to hit a lower unemployment rate.

Prime Minister Tony Abbott is promising to create one million jobs in the first five years of the Coalition Government and two million jobs over 10 years.

One cheer to that!

It is a promise that the drover's dog could deliver given the fact that Australia's population will be approximately two million larger in five years and four million larger in 10. All Mr Abbott is promising is to find half of the additional Australians a job. Even if he meets his first target of one million jobs in five years, the unemployment rate could well be around the 6 per cent, depending on the assumptions one may wish to make about future participation rates.

No one dares mention a target for the unemployment rate. The reasons for this obfuscation are reasonably straightforward.

If the participation rate falls a little and one million jobs are created, the unemployment rate will be about 5 to 5.5 per cent. If the participation rate rises, the unemployment rate will be at 6 per cent or higher and the number of people unemployed will be approximately 850 000.

No one dares mention a target for the unemployment rate.

See that? One million new jobs over five years would still leave around 850 000 people, and potentially 6 per cent of the labour force, unemployed. Hardly the stuff of economic success or a sign of bold and worthwhile economic policy reform.

As an aside, it should be noted that because of demographic trends, especially the ageing population, the labour force participation rate is forecast to trend lower over the next two to three decades.

On many other matters vital to the economy and policy management, there is bipartisan support for some specific targets. The most obvious example is the target for the RBA to have annual inflation held at 2 to 3 per cent over the business cycle. There are also targets on balancing the budget, or indeed running a small budget surplus over the economic cycle. Within that, there are targets for growth in real government spending, for the tax-to-GDP ratio to be anchored at a particular level and so on.

Yet no one dares mention a target for the unemployment rate.

If we are to have an unemployment rate target, how low (or high) should it be? If the target were to be, say, 4 per cent, some critics would say '4 per cent is still around 600 000 people—what a miserable ambition!'. To achieve such a low target, the structure of the Australian economy would need to change. Even if those changes were delivered, it would take many years — perhaps even decades — to deliver a structurally lower unemployment rate.

Education, skills and training, across the spectrum of the population from kindergarten kids to displaced middle-aged factory workers, need to be part of a vibrant and far-reaching skills and education platform. When young adults are ready to tackle paid employment, now and in the future, they will need to have the skill sets for a modern, high-income economy.

At a different level, when a middle-aged worker is threatened with unemployment as the industry they are in declines or is overtaken by offshore competitors, a retraining and re-skilling program is needed to ensure there is a strong probability that they can re-enter the workforce rather than being condemned to subsist on unemployment benefits for the rest of their life.

Some of the current unemployed are unfortunately close to unemployable in Australia's modern, advanced economy. This is because either they never had the skills or education to allow them to undertake work in an economy like Australia or the skills they built up early in their working life are now redundant and have not been updated or modified due to either poor public policy priorities or, in some cases, personal choice.

It is vital that the current degree of flexibility in our labour market be maintained. Wages need to be high enough to see workers maintain their attachment to the labour market and thereby help keep the participation rate at the highest possible level. At the same time, wages that are too high may crimp company profits and discourage companies from hiring additional staff as their businesses grow.

Australia should embrace a target for the unemployment rate and return to the policies that will see a sustainable move to, say, 4 per cent as a first step. It will require bold and well-targeted policy changes that are well known. And once 4 per cent is achieved and locked in, let's go for 3.5 per cent, even if it takes a long time to get there.

Australia should embrace a target for the unemployment rate and return to the policies that will see a sustainable move to, say, 4 per cent as a first step.

It should go without saying that the economy matters to everyone, no matter their age, location, occupation, wealth or position in life. Australia is a great country with a great economy that has had some good luck and generally good economic management over the past three decades.

Wealth and income levels have grown strongly over the past two decades. To maintain that degree of prosperity, it is important to pay attention to the economic news, taking note of changes in financial markets and policy settings from the RBA and the government. These changes will matter to you even if you feel there is little if anything you can do to influence them. You need to be aware of the changes to your financial risks and opportunities as policies and events evolve.

With even a little more knowledge and understanding of our economy, your ability to seize opportunities and minimise the negatives will no doubt greatly enhance your financial position. That has to be a good thing.

KEY POINTS

- The economy and the economic cycle are the fundamental drivers of your business and investments.
- Interest rates change, so be aware that at some stage over the life of your loan they will be higher than they are today.
- Policies also change, not just with a different party in government but also within the term of a government. Watch for those policy changes.
- Governments will be striving for budget surpluses, which means higher taxes are likely, as will be cuts to a range of government services. Be aware of what they may be.
- We are experiencing a big cycle right now: the unwinding of the terms of trade and mining investment boom. How far the terms of trade and with it Australia's national income falls remains to be seen, but beware of the risks for Australia if the decline is even more severe than currently envisaged.
- The unemployment rate is a critical indicator for the economy, but one that is little watched, managed or targeted as critical for growth.

chapter three
YOUR HOME AND MORTGAGE

Around two-thirds of the adult population have had or currently have a mortgage to buy the house or dwelling they live in. In other words, they have relied on debt to make the purchase of what is not only a lifestyle choice but also a path to financial security. That two-thirds proportion has not changed all that much over the decades, as many people enjoy the financial and 'psychological' benefits of spending money on a house via savings and a mortgage rather than spending money on rent that really only gives you a roof over your head, no matter how nice the house is.

To buy or to rent?

While buying a house to live in has proven to be a wonderful source of wealth creation over many decades, this seems to play only a minor part in most people's desire to borrow money and buy their own home.

The non-financial or psychological benefits are vitally important. Owning a home gives certainty as to where you will live over the long term, with no pesky landlord around to end your lease if you are a renter. Homeowners can do whatever they want to their home, unlike renters, who are constrained by the conditions of the lease. As an owner, you can paint your home whatever colour you wish, spend money on renovations, making it a more pleasant place to live in, and enjoy the benefits of setting up a garden and watching it grow as the years pass by. You can keep a pet, which is an option denied to many renters through the rental conditions set by most landlords. It is important to realise, as many people do, that in addition to the life-enhancing benefits of renovations to the kitchen, the outdoor living area, the lovely garden and the like, these improvements add value to your housing asset in advance of the day the house is sold and those gains are realised. And, quite incredibly, those gains are tax free.

In addition to the flexibility and other satisfactions associated with home ownership, the financial aspects of stepping up and buying a house are critically important.

After 20 years of renting, you have no housing assets at all. It is as simple as that. But after 20 years of owning and maintaining a mortgage, you have a valuable asset, even on the very conservative assumption that prices do not rise much over time. Certainly it is generally more expensive to buy a house than to rent (this is covered further in the pages ahead), but the benefits of having been forced to save to buy the house and then of 20 years of owning this asset are clear.

Holding off a house purchase on the expectation that prices will fall is fraught with financial danger.

There is probably no 'right' or 'wrong' time to buy a house to live in, if you are doing it for the right reasons and are prudent in the financial commitment you make when deciding to buy. For every warning that house prices are set to fall, so hold off a while before buying, there are stories of missed opportunities as house prices unexpectedly but inexorably move higher. Holding off a house purchase on the expectation that prices will fall is fraught with financial danger.

If you are wrong and while you are waiting house prices actually increase even an extra 5 per cent on a $600 000 property, that attempt to be too clever by half and pick the market timing has cost you $30 000 of after-tax money. If, on the other hand, you had stepped up, bought the house and prices fell 5 per cent (often seen as a worst-case scenario), who cares! It is of little relevance given you are not about to sell it to lock in that loss. You are living in your house and enjoying it. Over the next 10 or 15 years or more, prices will probably move higher, and in that time you will have paid off some of the debt and no doubt undertaken improvements to your house and made it a nicer place to live. A one-off 5 per cent price fall will be swamped by these long-run influences.

It is difficult to imagine that anyone who bought an average house anywhere in Australia 10 or more years ago has lost money. They simply haven't.

And over, say, a 10-year period, house prices rarely fall. So a price dip here or there should not be an issue, even if you bought the house near the top of the market. You bought it to live in and you plan to stay there for many years. In other words, purchasing a house for you to live in should be—must be—a long-term commitment. Paying 'too much' now probably won't matter much, if at all, even if annual house price gains over the next decade are moderate. Even annual house price gains of only 3 per cent, roughly half of the average price increases of the past three decades, will provide a financial benefit to you. It is difficult to imagine that anyone who bought an average house anywhere in Australia 10 or more years ago has lost money. They simply haven't.

If you see a house you like and can afford it, just buy it and don't hang around hoping for a price fall that probably will not happen.

There are lots of other issues often overlooked when weighing up whether to buy or to rent. The owner of a house has to pay local council rates and insurance, and cover the cost of repairs and maintenance for the hot-water system, carpets, painting, roof leaks, body corporate fees and the like. Most of these costs are part of the depreciation of the physical asset—the house—and are estimated to be around 2.5 to 3 per cent per year of the value of the house (excluding land). Even on a relatively inexpensive house this depreciation is around $5000 a year, and obviously it will be much higher for bigger and better houses. A house where the bricks, mortar, paint and fittings cost $400 000, for example, depreciates by around $10 000 a year. This cost is borne by the owner and not a renter.

Renters, while exposed to uncertainty about tenure, 'dead money' rent payments, the lack of picture hooks in the wall and living with that purple feature wall, at least do not have these costs to cover. They can also move house without the huge costs faced by a house owner, who must cough up the vast amounts required for stamp duty, real estate agent selling fees, advertising, legal fees and the like. Renters never have these expenses to worry about when they move.

A recent RBA study concluded that, in financial terms, it is close to break-even when comparing the costs of buying with renting a house. The key factor determining which is more financially desirable is the pace of house price gains needed to cover the extra costs of owning a house. Indeed, the unimproved value of a house needs to rise at a compound annual rate around 4 per cent to break even with the financial position of a renter, although it must be highlighted that this calculation does not take account of those psychological benefits mentioned.

In financial terms, it is close to break-even when comparing the costs of buying with renting a house.

That said, most people in Australia want to buy their own home. It seems they reckon the financial returns are reasonable to good over the longer run, and then there are those non-financial aspects that are so vitally important for wellbeing and enjoyment of life.

Even a nice garden can add $50 000 and more to the value of a house, although the cost of establishing one is well short of that amount. And not only is there a financial benefit, but you get to enjoy the garden every day you live there.

Many years of high house price growth have created a lot of wealth for those who bought their house 10, 15 or 20 and more years ago. For them, house price increases are nothing but good news.

That is all well and good for those who bought their house 10 or 20 years ago, but the current level of house prices has seen a lot of young people and other first-home buyers priced out of the housing market. There is a requirement for a large deposit, normally 20 per cent. For dwelling prices in the $300 000, $400 000 and $500 000 brackets, this requires a huge saving effort. Without the 20 per cent deposit, the banks will insist on very expensive mortgage insurance or will simply not grant the loan. Added to that 20 per cent deposit is the inevitably high debt level for the mortgage to cover the remaining 80 per cent or so of the purchase price.

The current high prices confirm that it is tough, financially, to meet all of the monetary requirements in order to get your foot in the door of the housing market.

Housing price trends and drivers

Contributing factors for persistently high house prices throughout most of Australia include these simple facts:

- Land is scarce relative to demand in the desirable parts of the major cities. Economics works! Strong growth in demand in concert with subdued growth in supply leads to higher prices, whether for bananas, iron ore or houses.
- Strong population growth in Australia, driven by high immigration inflows and natural increase, is the key driver of new demand. Whether these 'new Australians' rent or buy, they contribute to a higher demand for housing.
- An extended period of under-building of dwellings has been due in part to zoning and land restrictions and in part to poorly coordinated land release into new suburbs on the urban fringe of major cities. These regulatory issues limit the extent that, and the speed by which, the supply side of the economy can react to the unrelenting increases in demand. It needs to be highlighted that freeing up land in areas where no one wants to live is not a solution to supply. People want to be near their work, school, shops, public transport, hospitals or other amenities.
- A structural lowering of interest rates some 20 years ago fuelled a rise in the borrowing capacity of most mortgagees. Low interest rates mean that people can increase the amount of their mortgage — and therefore the price they are willing to bid on a house — without impact on the proportion of their income that they are using to pay for their mortgage, even if there are only moderate rises in their income.

- Australia is a rich country that enjoys high incomes. Most things, including houses, are expensive in rich countries.
- For owner-occupiers there is no capital gains tax, and this provides a huge incentive for people to maximise the value of the house they buy.

These key factors are likely to remain influential for some time to come, and this will keep a floor under house price levels in Australia. Accordingly, the issue of affordability for first-home buyers is also likely to persist for quite a few more years even if there is a push, via city planning, for better targeted land release and infrastructure spending to allow for housing supply to increase so the extra demand can be met.

Market trends have a habit of 'surprising' the experts, which is another way of saying that no one knows what the future holds.

Markets and specific economic issues are nearly impossible to forecast accurately in terms of the timing of a turning point or the order of magnitude of any change in a trend. Market trends have a habit of 'surprising' the experts (the lead into the global financial crisis, for example, was missed by just about all central bankers and most working in financial markets), which is another way of saying that no one knows what the future holds. This applies to house prices as much as it does to all other markets such as stocks, bonds, currencies and commercial property.

The fundamental drivers of house prices at the moment suggest a period of more moderate price increases or even a period when house prices move more or less sideways for an extended time. Nevertheless, there are various scenarios that could see house prices fall.

The following facts are not presented to alarm you but to outline the fact that house prices don't always go up. Occasionally they can fall and fall sharply. Very sharply.

Let's look around the globe over the past decade or so.

London in the mid 2000s had strong upward price pressures based on issues similar to those we see in Australia. These included housing shortages with little new building, scarce land, rising population and high demand. Yet house prices fell by a thumping 20 per cent between 2007 and 2009. This huge fall caused house owners, and the banks that lent to fund the mortgages, to lose a lot of money. Arguably, it was the very reason the GFC exploded in the United Kingdom, which in turn fuelled an economic collapse that on many measures matched the economic horrors of the 1930s Great Depression.

The reasons for the house price falls were clearly not supply and demand driven. Rather, they were linked to a tightening in credit by heavily indebted mortgage holders, and this was compounded by the fallout from the global financial crisis that spread from the United States to hit the banking sector in the United Kingdom.

In Ireland, at this time, house prices fell by more than 50 per cent, while nationwide in the US house prices fell over 30 per cent, with some cities and regions recording falls of around 60 per cent. These figures are truly devastating for the mortgage holder, for the banks and for policymakers trying to manage the economy and to craft policies that promote sustained solid growth in the economy.

Perhaps the starkest example of falling land prices occurred in central Tokyo in the late twentieth century. Having peaked in the late 1980s asset boom, by 2002 land prices had dropped 80 per cent—yes, 80 per cent!—as a rolling recession and chronic asset price deflation hit the Japanese economy. It is incredible what high debt and an unforeseen tightening in credit can do to house prices if unfavourable demographics and a poor policy response are also in play.

So, take a seat and think about the following scenario for Australian house prices—well, Sydney house prices in particular.

Imagine the consequences for you, your bank and the whole economy if you (along with tens of thousands of others) bought a house for $1 million, then over the next decade the value dropped $800 000 to just $200 000. Houses that were $500 000 would now be worth $100 000, while the $300 000 property would now be worth $60 000.

For the homeowner (multiplied by the effect on the whole economy), the impact would be dire. Horrible. There would be forced sales, bankruptcies and decimated savings. Many would have to hand over their keys to the banks. Banks would be all but insolvent (they would probably *be* technically insolvent) and would require government and taxpayer bailouts to keep their doors open. For the economy, unemployment would skyrocket, people would be without cash, savings would be eroded, business would not invest, and a long and deep recession would almost inevitably result.

Just look at the UK, Japan, the US and Ireland to see what happens to the economy when house prices boom and then rapidly bust. Not good.

It is instructive to examine how and why these house prices fell in economies that are similar in structure to Australia's in order to assess whether it could ever happen in Australia.

A critical component of most house price collapses in various parts of the world in recent years has been a sharp increase in house prices and housing debt *before* the bubble burst. House prices rose to bubble proportions in the US, UK and Europe owing to a mix of easy credit, poor regulation of lenders, very low interest rates, easy money and bandwagon buying, particularly by investors looking for a quick capital gain. Slack lending criteria from the banks (lending 100 per cent or more of the value of a property to just about anyone, regardless of their income), together with generally positive fundamentals, resulted in short supply and high demand for houses.

Right now in Australia in 2015 only a couple of price bubble characteristics are in place. Accordingly, a period of moderate price gains or even flat house prices is much more likely than a house price collapse.

Certainly, Australia's house prices have been 'high', 'elevated' or 'strong'—choose your descriptor. Interestingly, the bulk of the recent price increases followed a period when prices actually fell. This means that prices in Australia now are not bubble-like, even if they are high. The falls that occurred in Australia to deflate some of the current bubble risks were not huge, and between the end of 2010 and early 2012 house prices Australia-wide dropped by around 8 per cent. This context shows the recent gains in prices to be less impressive and less like the precursor to the house price busts in other countries.

In Australia in 2015 a period of moderate price gains or even flat house prices is much more likely than a house price collapse.

It is revealing to note that Australian house prices at the end of 2014 were only around 14 per cent above 2010 levels (see figure 3.1). This translates to an average annual increase of around 3.5 per cent over the past four years. Indeed, if we look only at Perth, Brisbane, Adelaide, Canberra and Hobart, house prices are broadly flat or even a little lower than there were four to five years ago. The big rise in house prices in more recent times has been centred on Sydney, with strong but less 'bubbly' price gains seen in Melbourne.

Figure 3.1: housing prices in Australian cities

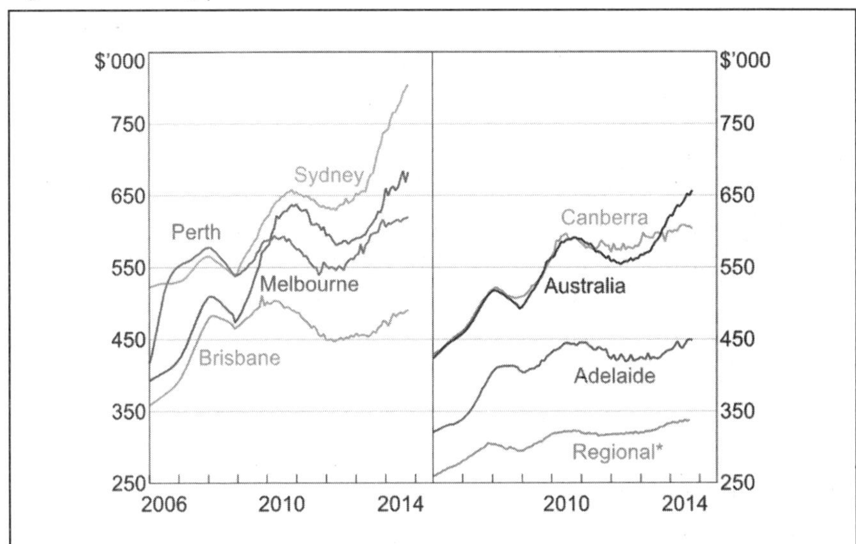

Source: © RP Data Pty Ltd 2015; © Reserve Bank of Australia 2001–2015.

Total house price gains for the past four or five years are not that much more than the rate of inflation. In the weaker cities, real house prices have actually fallen quite sharply, taking into account that the rate of inflation over the past five years has been a cumulative 13 per cent. Even for Sydney, the very recent price boom followed a period — from 2003–04 to 2008–09 — when prices were broadly flat.

Another issue that suggests a house price bubble is not evident in Australia is the fact that mortgage providers — mainly the big four banks — have tightened the criteria on which they lend. One benefit of the change to bank behaviour in the post-GFC climate is that banks now realise that it is not good practice to lend an amount at, or close to, the full price of the property, with scant regard to the income-earning history of the prospective borrower. In other words, the banks have made it more difficult for someone with a poor to mediocre credit history to borrow too much money relative to their income for a mortgage. At the same time, the banks have lowered the loan-to-valuation ratio criteria for even solid and creditworthy borrowers. As a consequence, annual housing credit growth in recent years has been about 5 to 7 per cent compared with an average of around 15 per cent in much of the 1990s and 2000s.

Bank loan arrears, bad debts and non-performing assets for housing remain near historical lows. In other words, very few people are defaulting on their mortgages, even given the very slight uptick during the GFC.

While mortgage debt remains very high, and there has been a disproportionate lift in borrowing specifically for housing investment purposes in the past couple of years, it appears that the general quality of that lending has been reasonably sound. As a result, bank loan arrears, bad debts and non-performing assets for housing remain near historical lows (see figure 3.2). In other words, very few people are defaulting on their mortgages, even given the very slight uptick during the GFC.

Figure 3.2: banks' non-performing assets (bad debts)

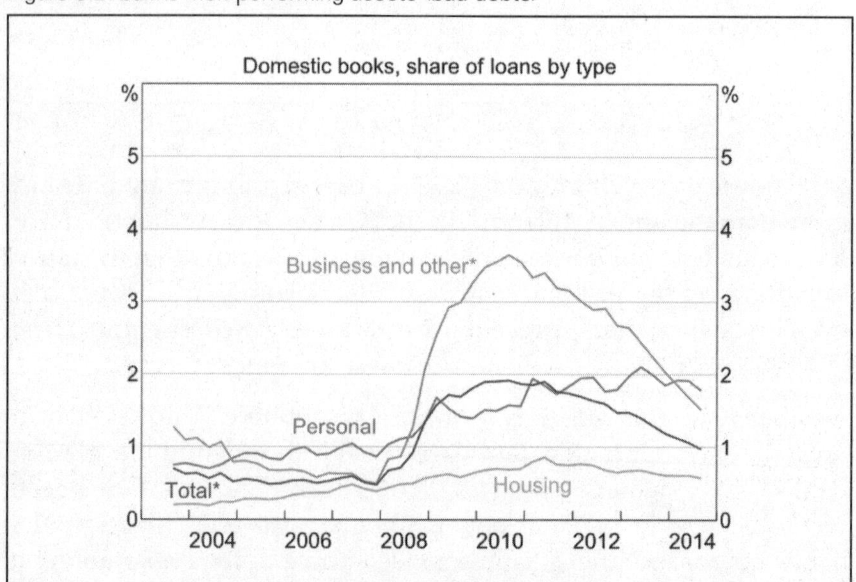

Source: © Australian Prudential Regulation Authority 2015.

There are a couple of areas that make Australian house prices vulnerable to sharp falls over the next few years. If there is an extended period of economic weakness brought about by the fall in commodity prices and terms of trade, incomes will fall and the highly indebted consumer will be at risk of unemployment or lower wages.

On the supply and demand side, there are some tentative signs of rising supply from high levels of new dwelling construction, while the recent immigration data show some slowing, albeit from a high starting point, in the number of new permanent arrivals. If Australia sees a sustained pickup in new construction at a time when population growth slows, the supply and demand imbalances — and house price pressures — could reverse.

There are, for the moment, more downside than upside risks to house prices. A likely scenario is that in the next few years the house price exuberance will fade, with a period of flat to slightly lower prices more likely than not.

Mortgage interest rates

Of course, the three absolutely vital elements to consider when buying a house are its price, your income and interest rates. There isn't much more that will determine whether you can afford that house, with a mortgage or not.

Interest rates will undoubtedly be a major influence on demand for credit and new borrowing, as potential purchasers of real estate check their monthly repayments relative to their income under various interest rate scenarios. Not only is today's interest rate important in these calculations, but when the loan is considered, borrowers should do some scenario planning. This means calculating the interest cost to take account of the possibility that interest rates will rise from the level in place when the loan is taken out. Given the impossibility of forecasting interest rates over one year, let alone 3, 5 or 10 years over the course of the loan, it is wise to see how tough things would be for the household budget if interest rates are 2 or even 3 per cent higher than today.

If the borrower fails to do this, the banks and other mortgage providers should do it on their behalf to make sure that they, the banks, minimise problem loans on their books should interest rates rise in the years over which the mortgage is taken out.

Over the past decade, the standard variable mortgage interest rate has averaged around 7.2 per cent — it has been as low as 5.0 per cent and as high as 9.6 per cent. While no one is seriously contemplating that the RBA will hike interest rates to a point that sees the mortgage rate approach that recent high, it is safe to assume that at some stage over the course of a 25-year mortgage, interest rates will spend about as much time above 7 per cent as below. It is worth keeping that in mind when you look at the current low mortgage rates and the size of your loan.

The experience of the past few years of super-low mortgage interest rates (well below 6 per cent) is linked inexorably to global economic circumstances. This has seen most of the world's major central banks — the US Federal Reserve, the European Central Bank, the Bank of Japan, the Bank of England, the Bank of Canada and others — slash interest rates to near zero as they try to revive their economies in the post-GFC period of economic funk.

While Australia has not had a recession, these low global interest rates have forced the RBA to set Australian rates at record lows as a result of the fallout from still sub-optimal economic growth globally, but also to take some of the heat out of what was an extraordinary valuation for the Australian dollar — it peaked at US$1.10 in 2011.

The recent collapse in commodity prices is another driver of Australia's incredibly low interest rates. It means that mining investment is falling, national income growth is being scaled back and the downside risks to the medium-term economic growth outlook have intensified. The RBA has set interest rates at low levels to guard against anything sinister unfolding in the economy and to try to engineer stronger growth in the local economy to offset some of the weakness coming from overseas.

The recent collapse in commodity prices is another driver of Australia's incredibly low interest rates.

The path back to what might be considered 'normal' interest rates — that is, rates that are higher than now and nearer the long-run averages — will be protracted and uneven. So bad is the economic hangover from the GFC that many central banks in industrialised countries are treading very cautiously when it comes to adjusting their super-easy stance on monetary policy. Some are even ramping up monetary policy easing with negative interest rates—yes, *negative* interest rates. In the Eurozone things are that grim. It seems that central banks, including the US Federal Reserve, fear repeating the mistake of the 1930s Great Depression, when after a little good news economic policy was tightened. Back then this proved to be premature, and by taking away the easy policy settings too early it prolonged and deepened the period of economic malaise that only really ended after the Second World War.

WHAT ARE NEGATIVE INTEREST RATES?

Following is an extract from a column I wrote for Business Spectator *in 2012:*

Throughout Europe and in Japan the interest rates paid on government bond yields have dipped into negative territory. These record low-interest rates from both the bond market and central banks are a proper and natural reaction to chronically weak economic growth, mass unemployment and disinflation—a period of falling inflation.

The concept of negative interest rates is a real brain-teaser. Economics textbooks do not mention them, let alone analyse the consequences of such a market move.

Intuitively, one would judge that lenders must receive a positive return (interest) to lend their money to a borrower, and the borrower must pay (interest) for the privilege of holding and using that money.

With negative interest rates, it's as though you hire a car and not only do you get the car to drive around for free, but the car hire company gives you $50 because you are a good, reliable and low-risk customer and they are confident you will return the car in good shape and on time. Substitute 'money' for 'car' and that is what is happening in some bond markets with negative interest rates.

Negative rates mean the lender—in this instance a bank or a fund manager—agrees to forgo some of the principal to hold the paper issued by the government. One reason they do this is because they have a high level of confidence that the remaining 99.5 per cent or so of the principal will be repaid. (With positive interest rates of 0.5 per cent, the lender would get back 100.5 per cent of the principal at the maturity of the loan.)

(continued)

WHAT ARE NEGATIVE INTEREST RATES? *(cont'd)*

Another reason why negative interest rates are becoming more widespread is because banks and other investors see no alternative creditworthy investments. If there were low-risk and creditworthy alternatives, the money would be allocated to those markets rather than being locked up with slowly eroding value due to negative yields.

These facts only reinforce how grim economic conditions have been throughout the Eurozone and Japan.

There is also the question of how negative interest rates actually occur. Surely it would be better just to hold cash? At least a ten-euro note is worth €10 in two years' time, unlike a negative interest rate bond, which will be worth less than €10 when it matures.

The proposition of holding physical cash falls down when the size of the market involved is considered. The fund managers and banks have tens of billions of euros and francs to invest. They cannot physically hold the notes and coins in cash and they do not want to place their money with a bank for fear that the counterparty bank will default. That's when you lose 100 per cent of your money. When the funds are allocated to the safe-haven of government bonds, the interest rate is pushed lower and lower until it goes negative. It is as simple as that.

In the current economic climate, the global economy is likely to register reasonable rates of growth in the next few years as the slow repair continues. In some countries, such as the US, the UK and Canada, where interest rates may edge up as growth and job creation build further, the rises are unlikely to be as aggressive as the cuts that were delivered as the GFC hit.

In the current economic climate, the global economy is likely to register reasonable rates of growth in the next few years as the slow repair continues.

Interest rates in the Eurozone and Japan are likely to remain very low for years to come, which will likely influence global borrowing costs including those associated with your mortgage.

Given these factors, interest rates in Australia are likely to remain low in the near term, and the fall in the terms of trade, the weak labour market and low wages and inflation mean the RBA should keep rates at or near levels never before seen. But at the first sniff of a turn in the economic indicators, if the US Federal Reserve follows through with an interest rate hiking cycle and some form of stability returns to the Eurozone and Japan, there will of course be scope — and in fact a need — for the RBA to ponder interest rate hikes over the medium term or, say, two to five years hence.

Which goes back to the point first made in chapter 1 — that it matters greatly to us in Australia what happens in the US economy, the Eurozone and India, Chinese demand for commodities, and other global economic and market events. All of these factors will impact on our economy and, of course, local policymakers.

My point is that when looking to take on a mortgage for your lifestyle and financial investment, you must — I repeat *must* — factor in the risk that interest rates could, and probably will at some stage, be a good deal higher than when you take out that loan. The comforting thing is that in doing this, if for some unforeseen reason interest rates do not in fact rise as much as you factor into your worst-case scenario, or indeed they stay low or fall, then you will either have spare cash in your pocket or you will be paying off your loan considerably faster than the standard 25-year duration of most variable mortgages.

When looking to take on a mortgage for your lifestyle and financial investment, you must *factor in the risk that interest rates could, and probably will at some stage, be a good deal higher than when you take out that loan.*

The benefits of careful planning have been evident in the past three or four years, during which interest rates have fallen to levels that virtually no one could have foreseen. If you took out a mortgage at any stage in the past few years and planned for the possibility of higher interest rates, you are much better off than you expected. Either you are well ahead in your repayment schedule or you have reduced the principal of the loan faster than anticipated or you have extra cash.

It pays to be prudent.

THE FLOATING VERSUS FIXED-RATE MORTGAGE

One critical question for those with a mortgage or looking to take on a mortgage is: which is better — a floating interest rate or one that is fixed for a number of years?

Usually the question is couched in terms of possible savings — what rate is likely to be lower? In my view, this is only a small part of why someone would consider a floating or fixed mortgage.

Given that it is not possible to accurately forecast or anticipate interest rate changes over a period of several years, the decision to float or to fix needs to take account of other considerations. By fixing your mortgage, you are effectively speculating that the floating interest rate over the term of that loan will be higher than the rate you have locked in with the fixed-rate mortgage. You might have done the right thing, but you might not if, in fact, interest rates fall.

The key consideration when choosing a floating or fixed-rate mortgage has more to do with financial security than speculation. If, like many people, you prefer to know exactly how much your monthly mortgage repayment will be over the next three or five years, take out a fixed-rate mortgage. That way you know that every month, regardless of what happens to official interest rates, your repayment will be fixed at a specific dollar amount.

A floating rate mortgage, of course, changes with movements in the RBA official interest rate but also is open to change when the banks' cost of funds changes due to market conditions. A floating-rate mortgage has the benefits of riding this cycle down as well as up, and unlike most fixed-rate mortgages, floating-rate mortgages allow you to make lump-sum payments off the principal and increase your repayments if you are lucky enough to get a cash windfall or a pay rise.

So, floating or fixed? If you like certainty, then fixed; if you are happy to ride the interest rate cycle and reckon you might get some extra cash via pay rises or some other means, go floating.

Taking the plunge

Delaying the purchase of a house to live in based on the hope that prices will soon fall has other hazards. It merely pushes back the question of saving and managing your mortgage to later years. Taking the plunge and buying your house with what is invariably going to be a large mortgage, and entering the world of forced savings via your mortgage, as you approach retirement you will want to be in a position where the mortgage debt has been paid off.

Taking the plunge to buy your first house (or apartment) at age 25 to 30 should mean you are more likely to have full ownership of your house by age 65 than someone who waits until they are 30 to 35 to step into the housing market. It might be that you don't get your dream house first off and you must wait a while for that pleasure.

You probably don't want to get to 65 and still have a mortgage because it took you so long to bite the bullet and buy your first house. On the contrary.

Those reaching 55, 60 or 65 at the latest who have paid off that mortgage after years of hard financial slog will have a vital aspect of their financial security locked in. The benefits of paying off a house before those twilight years are obvious, or at least they should be. You can retire or plan for retirement knowing you will never have to make a mortgage repayment or pay rent ever again. Never. How good would that be, especially if you have also tucked away some cash in your superannuation fund.

Those reaching 55, 60 or 65 at the latest who have paid off that mortgage after years of hard financial slog will have a vital aspect of their financial security locked in.

Indeed, the money you earn from work in your pre-retirement years or from your superannuation savings is *all* yours if you don't have a mortgage or rent to pay. There is also the option of downsizing your house or moving to somewhere that is less expensive and cheaper to maintain. This would mean selling your house (on which all capital gains and improvements are tax free) and gaining some spare cash to do whatever you want with once you move into smaller or less expensive digs. What a nice thing to be dealing with for those lucky or smart enough to get into the house-buying market early in their lives.

Reverse mortgages

The other benefit of early home ownership is certainty. You can stay put for as long as you want — the house is yours. If you are asset rich, with your house owned outright, and income poor, if you have retired and are living off superannuation or a government pension, you have the option of taking out a reverse mortgage and using the collateral of your house to fund your consumption in retirement.

A reverse mortgage is an arrangement in which the owner of the house accrues a regular payment from the bank and, over time, a mortgage debt accumulates. It is the opposite of getting a huge lump-sum loan and slowly repaying it — hence 'reverse' mortgage. Of course, the bank charges interest on this money as it is forwarded to you and as the debt increases over time by the payments to you plus interest.

When you die and the house is sold by the beneficiaries of your estate, the bank is paid out the final amount owing (all of the payments to you plus interest) and the remainder is paid to your estate.

The following example shows how a reverse mortgage can work.

Assume your house is worth $1 million and you are 70 years old. You need a little extra cash each month so you arrange for a payment from the bank (the reverse mortgage) of, say, $1000 a month. That $1000 will help cover your bills and allow you to do some nice things, as it comes on top of your superannuation or pension income.

Let's assume you die at age 80, meaning you have had the reverse mortgage for 10 years with an average interest rate of 6 per cent. The amount of the loan accrued via the reserve mortgage will be around $190 000. Even if the house you are still living in and enjoying in retirement does not change at all in value over that decade and stays at $1 million, when you die your beneficiaries will receive over $800 000 from the house. The good part is that you would have had that bit of extra money each month in your twilight years.

If perchance your house has risen in value at a very conservative annual rate of 3 per cent, your beneficiaries will be selling a house worth around $1.38 million. So after your debt has been repaid, they get to pocket around $1.2 million from the property, even though you have drawn down $1000 a month for 10 years. If house prices rise at, say, 5 per cent per annum, in a decade your house will be worth more than $1.6 million, leaving your benefactors with $1.4 million.

Having a house that you own gives you the flexibility to do many things to help make yourself financially secure in retirement.

Certainly this is a very simplified version. You may wish to increase the drawdown over time to keep up with the cost of living increases that will occur through inflation, or you may live longer, or there could be a myriad of other issues. But the story is clear: having a house that you own gives you the flexibility to do many things to help make yourself financially secure in retirement.

THE GENEROUS PARENT/GRANDPARENT

Okay, not everyone was born with parents or grandparents who are financially well off. But a lot of people were, and this is where some intergenerational fairness can come in. We see it in stories of people paying for their grandchildren's education or giving them a deposit for their first home.

With all of the wealth that older people have in their home, investments and superannuation, why don't more of them gift what would be a fraction of that wealth as a house deposit for their grandchildren? With high house price gains over the past few decades and ridiculously favourable tax treatment for superannuation holders, many well-off older people could comfortably give their children or grandchildren a helping hand in getting into the property market.

Think of the thrill of making a gift that brings their savings up to that magical 20 per cent deposit? For you and the recipient. Let's face it. Your children will get the money when you die, so why wait? See the joy and relief in their eyes when you hand over that financial boost.

Early inheritance? Yes, it probably is, but at least you get to see the money going into a wonderful asset — a home.

Despite their obvious virtues, reverse mortgages are not all that popular. Ageing homeowners fear they will use up all of the value of their house or leave less of a financial legacy for their beneficiaries. The potential beneficiaries may not be too thrilled with the prospect of their inheritance being eroded when the reverse mortgage option is pursued by an asset-rich but income-poor retiree.

Be that as it may, the case for reverse mortgages is sound in the right circumstances. And it is an option available only to those who own their home, which is the point about buying and paying off your house as soon as possible.

Affordability

The more these examples are considered, the stronger the case becomes for doing all you can to buy a house. Making the sacrifices to buy a house as soon as you can scrape together a deposit and get a manageable loan is worth it in the long run. And the earlier in life you get started on the property ladder, the better.

So beg, steal or borrow that deposit, be realistic in the property you wish to buy and go for it. This itself leads to the question that continues to dominate the thoughts of younger people as they look to enter the housing market: housing affordability.

Making the sacrifices to buy a house as soon as you can scrape together a deposit and get a manageable loan is worth it in the long run. And the earlier in life you get started on the property ladder, the better.

With house prices high by most measures and the banks being more cautious when it comes to lending more than 80 per cent of the value of a property, it is increasingly difficult for young people to step into the housing market, even if they are on a relatively good income, having finished school and university.

How can those first-home buyers, generally young people, break into the housing market when prices, and the deposit needed, are so high?

It is a question that has been asked for many decades. Without going into the full history of how difficult it has *always* been to get one's finances ready to buy that first house, it is important to highlight that the question of affordability is not solely linked to house price. Other vital factors that determine whether or not you can convince the bank to lend you the money you need to buy a house are your income and the level of interest rates.

It has always been difficult for first-home buyers to get their finances organised to qualify for a mortgage for the first time.

House prices have been growing at a strong pace over the past decade or two. So too have household incomes, especially in after-tax terms. The economic boom has seen two decades of real wage increases, which has helped, at least in part, to offset the elevated house price levels. That said, house price growth has outpaced income growth. This means that house prices, as a multiple of household incomes, are high, but curiously they are only at the upper end of the long-run average and no more. It is therefore fair to say that house prices are high but not intolerably so, at least based on the ratio of house price to household income.

Estimates show that housing takes about the same share of a household's after-tax income to service now as it has, on average, over the past 30 years.

But the house price-to-income ratio is only part of the affordability issue. Interest rates matter too. Over the past 20 to 30 years, there has been a clear long-run downtrend in interest rates. Since the late 1980s, the peaks and troughs in each interest rate cycle have been lower—that is, lower peaks in interest rate tightening cycles and lower lows in interest rate cutting cycles. This is unlikely to continue forever as the official interest rates set by the RBA get remarkably close to zero.

When judging housing, the perception that affordability is a greater obstacle today than ever before is wrong when we add interest rates and household incomes into the equation. Indeed, such estimates show that housing takes about the same share of a household's after-tax income to service now as it has, on average, over the past 30 years.

Indeed, the RBA estimates that since the mid 1980s the proportion of an average household's disposable income required for payment on the average standard loan (the debt servicing ratio of a mortgage) has hovered between 20 and 30 per cent, with only rare and very temporary marginal moves outside that range. That RBA estimate is based on a technical assumption that the mortgage has an 80 per cent loan-to-valuation ratio and is based on average household disposable income before interest payments.

The most recent estimate of the household mortgage debt servicing ratio on that basis is around 22 per cent—that is, it currently takes around 22 per cent of household disposable income to service an average mortgage. This is despite both house prices and the size of an average mortgage being very high. The reason for this low debt servicing cost is that household incomes have been growing at a solid pace over a long time frame and interest rates are now very low.

When I speak to people about this measure, they generally don't believe it. Surely, they say, the massive house price gains of recent decades mean people need to devote an ever-increasing proportion of their take-home pay to meet their mortgage obligations?

The answer is no. It was arguably harder 25 years ago in terms of the proportion of your disposable pay needed to pay off a mortgage than it is today.

It is this mix of variables—house prices, income and interest rates—that is likely to ensure that this most comprehensive measure of affordability remains within the bounds of comfort.

Think of housing affordability in this way.

In the mid to late 1980s, a house cost, say, \$75 000 and required a mortgage of \$60 000—that is, a loan-to-valuation ratio of 80 per cent. Household incomes at this time were around \$25 000 per annum and interest rates were around 13.5 per cent. In these circumstances, it took around 20 to 25 per cent of a household's after-tax income to make the monthly mortgage repayment. The other 75 per cent of disposable income could be spent as the householder wanted.

Fast forward to now. A house is around \$625 000 and, based on a loan-to-valuation ratio of 80 per cent, the mortgage would be around \$500 000. Household disposable income is around \$125 000 per annum and the interest rate is 5.25 per cent (although the increased competition now compared with the 1980s means that not many people pay this advertised rate). In these circumstances, it takes around 20 to 25 per cent of a household's after-tax income to make the monthly repayments.

While house prices are up, so too are household incomes and, critically, interest rates are structurally down.

This shows, quite starkly, that it is no tougher financially for a first-home buyer today to service an average mortgage on an average house than it was 20 or 30 years ago. It is just that in the so-called good old days, the average home buyer's mortgage pain came through interest rates and not the house price. Now, the pain comes through the house price and not interest rates and, I suspect, expectations being skewed to buying above-average houses.

Looking at it another way, monthly repayments are much the same on a $400 000 mortgage with an interest rate at 5.25 per cent as they are on a $300 000 mortgage with an interest rate of 8 per cent.

As a homeowner with a mortgage, what would you prefer? The joy of buying a house at a low price, with a relatively low mortgage, but having to pay a high interest rate, or taking out a large mortgage on an expensive house but having a low interest rate to service that loan?

Any prospective home buyer should be largely indifferent to these dynamics. Those wanting lower house prices, beware! It might come at the cost of higher interest rates, which would do little or nothing to help affordability.

Think of it this way. House prices could undoubtedly fall to make them more affordable, and a return to 8 per cent interest rates would no doubt help achieve that. Imagine paying a 13.5 per cent mortgage interest rate (as paid in the 1980s) right now. Obviously, if that were ever to occur again, a first-home buyer's delight in getting a cheaper house and therefore borrowing less would, by definition, be neutralised by the pain of higher interest rates.

For those bemoaning high house prices now by stressing the lack of affordability, go to one of those very good mortgage calculators that are so common on the internet. Plug 10 per cent, 13.5 per cent or even the 1990s peak of 17 per cent into the 'interest rate' box and see how much you could afford to borrow today. The exercise should change those perceptions of poor housing affordability in recent years.

I am not sorry for going on about this — it is a vital point to make. It is a roundabout way of saying that it has *never* been easy to get into the housing market for the first time or to upgrade to a nicer house, but it is no harder now than it was in the past. It is just that the dynamics and the mix are different.

What has not changed is that sacrifices need to be made to get your foot in the door of the property market.

It has never *been easy to get into the housing market for the first time or to upgrade to a nicer house, but it is no harder now than it was in the past. It is just that the dynamics and the mix are different.*

Sacrifices include directing your spending towards a mortgage and away from otherwise nice things to do. Make a choice on where you spend your money. That may mean taking less expensive holidays, eating less expensive food, driving a cheaper car — whatever it takes, as long as at the end of the day your savings allow you to meet the mortgage repayments.

Sorry, but while saving the deposit for a nice house and then making the monthly repayments plus upkeep costs may not be much fun, particularly in the early years of a loan, it's well and truly worth it.

Buying a house to live in is both desirable in itself and a financially sound thing to do. In addition to financial security over the decades into your middle age and then retirement, there are many non-financial benefits that make it a good idea.

I admit that taking that step from renting to entering the property market is rarely easy. It never has been. The point is you will find it is well worth the effort, especially over the course of 10 years or more. Along the way, of course there will be disconcerting swings in interest rates and some risk of house price falls. But over time it is likely, if not certain, that your wage will increase, which will help you meet the mortgage repayments, regardless of interest rates and the value of your property.

Which leads to another question to think about when you nervously sign those mortgage documents, fearing the level of debt you are about to incur.

Over the course of five years, most household incomes will increase by about 25 per cent, or a little under 5 per cent per annum. This takes account of normal wage increases of around 3 to 4 per cent per year plus, hopefully, promotions to more senior levels in the workforce. Over the five years your mortgage becomes relatively smaller, even if you have only paid interest and the principal is unchanged.

In this illustration, think of a household earning $100 000 a year with a $400 000 mortgage. In five years, the income will be $125 000 while the mortgage will still be $400 000 if you have only paid interest. It will be a little less (about $390 000) if your 25-year loan is interest and principal. In 10 years, the household income will be $160 000 and the amount outstanding on the mortgage will be about $325 000, depending on interest rates over that long-run period. Your loan-to-income ratio is now just above two, from being four when you took out the loan. And this takes no account of changes in house prices, which over a long time frame almost certainly go up.

You can see another issue here: it is that wages growth helps pay off your house. If we take account of house price rises, and we assume a very modest annual average increase of 3 per cent, your $500 000 dwelling today will be worth $580 000 in five years and $670 000 in ten.

I wind up this chapter with a few home truths about buying a house.

Location is important. Of course everyone wants to live in a 'good' area. One close to transport or work, or to the trendy cafés, shops and restaurants, maybe with ready access to schools, medical facilities, parks, the beach — whatever you and most other people see as desirable.

Obviously, properties in these 'good' areas are relatively expensive, or certainly more so than properties even a few kilometres away. It is that old supply and demand equation coming into play again. There is a limited supply of houses and land in 'nice' areas. While population and incomes grow, there will probably always be rising demand. Indeed, it seems inevitable that high demand relative to supply will always underpin prices in nice areas.

The harsh reality may be that you simply cannot afford to buy your first house in a more desirable area. This does not mean you don't buy a house to live in. If the inner-city terrace you adore is too expensive relative to your income, it means you buy somewhere else.

The harsh reality may be that you simply cannot afford to buy your first house in a more desirable area.

In late 2013, a terrifically talented journalist at *The Guardian*, Bridie Jabour, wrote a piece lamenting her inability to afford to live in one of these desirable areas. It was provocatively titled 'Not buying lattes won't help me buy a house'.

She made some excellent points about the affordability issue for potential first-home buyers like herself. She took issue with those — like me, I suppose — who suggested that the consumption patterns of young people (lattes, holidays, dinners out) meant they were choosing not to save for a house but instead to spend their money in other areas.

The following feature outlines my response to Ms Jabour's article. If you read nothing else closely in this book and you are wondering why you cannot afford your favoured house, read this.

FIRST-HOME BUYERS' CHOICES MEAN SOME WILL NEVER BUY

Ms Jabour laments that a house in the street where she lives sold for over $900 000 a few months ago. In disclosing this, she is telling readers she lives in an area where house prices are around 15 to 20 per cent above the median for Sydney. For a first-home buyer, that seems very ambitious.

It is difficult to imagine there being a first-home buyer that would not want to have their first home well above average, but they are competing with people who have the benefit of age, savings, job promotions and the like to have the ability to buy above-average property.

Picking a house 15 to 20 per cent *below* the median would mean a price some $275 000 cheaper than one 15 to 20 per cent above median. The financial issues associated with buying a $900 000 property versus one of $625 000 should be obvious.

Ms Jabour makes an error when she notes, 'Owning a home in a city like mine is as remote to me as getting a seat next to Lady Gaga on the first commercial space flight'. She should have said that owning a house in that 'street or suburb', rather than 'city', was the issue.

Ms Jabour then outlines some of her spending and saving patterns and calculates that she could save $58 400 over five years if she gave up going out and taking holidays. This amount possibly overstates her savings, as she notes, given the substitution of meals at home, for example, which is correct. I would simply note that the pool of savings would attract some interest to offset that.

Ms Jabour then very rightly notes the downside to renting. The dreaded inspections, the risk of being kicked out on the landlord's whim and not having the piece of mind of where she will be living in retirement. All these issues have some validity, and she could have added not being able to keep a pet (usually) or nail in hooks for pictures or change the garden and the like. But ignored are the onerous costs for homeowners (including landlords) of council rates, insurance and depreciation, which covers things like the hot-water system blowing up, fixing a leaking roof, laying a new carpet, painting and a new kitchen every 20 years or so. On an average house these will add around $7500 to $10 000 a year.

This is where Ms Jabour notes, 'I could maybe afford a house in the outer suburbs of Sydney'.

Bingo!

Because Ms Jabour says 'maybe', I get the impression she hasn't looked closely at the prices out there, many of which are around half those in her street, and probably without a leaking roof and crappy wardrobes.

I think, unintentionally, Ms Jabour has found the answer to her problems, but it is an answer she doesn't like. Moving to the outer suburbs means for Ms Jabour that she would 'want to give up everything that makes my life fun for five years'. Been there, done that.

Again, in a revelation about the problems, not joys, of owning a house, Ms Jabour highlights the burdens of stamp duty, pest tests, surveying costs and body corporate fees if it is a unit. It is indeed costly to buy a house, which lessens its attractiveness.

(continued)

FIRST-HOME BUYERS' CHOICES MEAN SOME WILL NEVER BUY *(cont'd)*

It is here that Ms Jabour makes the unsubstantiated claim that 'housing affordability is not a Generation Y issue, it's not even a Generation X issue. It's an issue for every single one of us not born rich'. It is unclear why Ms Jabour associates the 68 per cent of the population in Australia who own a house as being 'born rich'. I would like to see any background to that claim, but I suspect it is an error and that many people who own a house are on very modest incomes and were not born rich.

Ms Jabour remains off the mark by blaming 'people with ridiculous amounts of cash who see a sellers' market and buy up investment properties' as a reason for her perception of housing. I assume she includes her landlord in this statement? While investors can and have driven house prices higher and there is an excellent case for the abolition of negative gearing, it is a little too cute to blame those who provide rental property for the non-homeowners for their inability to buy a house. Indeed, it is clear that Ms Jabour is enjoying the returns of renting an above-average property without being able to afford to buy it.

And then, in the final few paragraphs, Ms Jabour hits a couple of nails on their heads.

Land release, negative gearing and capital gains tax on the family house — critical issues that have had an impact on house prices. Land release is the easy one, and this is something that must be addressed and all efforts to in-fill and provide decent infrastructure in new suburbs is to be encouraged. Negative gearing is another poor policy that should be abolished, and soon.

All up, Ms Jabour raises a range of valid issues that reiterate the decent point that affordable housing is a critical issue on equity grounds. That said, it is an issue that requires people to avoid turning up their nose if the affordable house is in a good location but of less than average quality or in a less desirable area but of a better standard.

There is the issue that land release will see the number of new dwellings increase, which should help dampen the house price gains. But, alas for Ms Jabour, these new dwellings will by definition be in the outer suburbs and away from the attractions she obviously values.

To help out, I then posted a list of properties in Sydney with a price around the $550 000 to $600 000 mark that seemed perfectly respectable but were perhaps not in the 'nice' area where prices were nearer $900 000.

This was a terrific interchange of ideas and perceptions about home ownership. It highlights that some have unrealistic expectations about the house they can buy and, indeed, the changes to their spending patterns needed if they are to accumulate a decent deposit and then have sufficient funds to service a mortgage.

Buying cheaper property may mean buying and living in a less desirable area. Or a smaller place with one less bedroom or bathroom. In every city and town, there are still lots of relatively inexpensive houses around—it is just that they tend to fall short of what some people want.

KEY POINTS

- Buying a house to live in is not only sensible for many personal reasons; it is also an excellent long-run financial proposition.
- It may not be easy to save the deposit for your first house, or to make the repayments every month, but with a few changes to your spending patterns you can no doubt do it.
- Set your expectations to a realistic level. Buy a house you can afford even if this means adjusting your expectations a little lower than your dream house.
- Buying a house to live in is a long-run decision. Don't fret if prices fall the year after you buy. You were not about to sell anyway, so enjoy your new lifestyle.
- Do interest rate scenario planning: whatever the interest rate is today, assume it will be two or even three percentage points higher later in your repayment period.
- Owning a house in retirement gives you a huge financial advantage, including the possibility of taking out a reverse mortgage if your other income is too low.
- Be realistic with your house purchase: don't stay out of the market because your dream home in the dream location is too expensive.

---

chapter four
YOUR BUSINESS

Running a business is rarely easy.

Many variables impact on sales, your costs, growth, suppliers, debt, staffing—and therefore profits. Many of the drivers that influence how well you do in your business are outside your control.

Chief among external influences is the overall performance of the economy. This should be obvious but is often overlooked by business owners. When consumers are tight for cash because of low wages growth or following a loss of confidence due to financial market ructions or poor policymaking from the government, they will be less inclined to spend. Indeed, they will be less *able* to spend unless they choose to run down savings or increase debt, neither of which is likely in a weak economy. This hurts your business. Worse still, if growing numbers of consumers are unemployed owing to a weak economy or, in the worst case, a recession, they cannot afford to spend any more than their subsistence income. All of which is bad news for your business.

The opposite is true in a time of strong economic and jobs growth, and when wages rise at a pace comfortably above the inflation rate. Consumers can, and inevitably do, spend more as their real incomes grow. It is a similarly positive scenario when the economy sustains an expansion that sees the unemployment rate fall and those now in paid employment starting to spend their wages. In this climate, businesses will be inclined to lift their capital expenditure, expanding their opportunities to take advantage of the favourable conditions.

These actions in themselves further boost economic activity as the new office block or warehouse is built, fitted with furniture and machinery, and of course filled with staff.

It is time to jettison the absurd obsession with the budget deficit/surplus that has held back decent policymaking over recent times.

Clearly, this is why it is critically important that government policymakers and the RBA 'get it right' when setting the framework for the economy to grow. Setting interest rates at a level that promotes sustainable growth consistent with the inflation target, framing the budget to support economic growth and jobs — these are vitally important measures. As for the budget, it is time to jettison the absurd obsession with the budget deficit/surplus that has held back decent policymaking over recent times.

Managing your business within the macroeconomy

The importance of the big economic picture for your business is also why each snippet of economic data and each report on evolving financial market trends makes the news. Helpfully, this economic reporting details the latest data and what they might mean for jobs, wages, interest rates, the Australian dollar and even the budget. All this, of course, has implications for your business.

A run of data that shows strong retail sales, a lift in building approvals, rising business investment and solid export growth would obviously be good news. It means your business is likely to be functioning during a strong growth period in which a dynamic economy prevails. This is especially so if the strong area — retail sales, for example — is your main area of operation. For housing, if you are in real estate, it would obviously be welcome news to see housing finance grow, with house prices moving upward and interest rates remaining low.

Unless you work in a firm involved with receivership or some related industry, it is clearly better for your business to be operating in a robust economy and seeing a sustained lift in spending, investment and employment. It is good also for the government to find itself presiding over a strong economy. This begs an obvious question: if a strong economy is so good, why doesn't the government, Treasury and the RBA aim to maximise growth all the time? Why do they sometimes implement very high interest rates or restrictive levels of government spending or higher taxes, all of which obviously slow the economy down?

Well, economic policymaking is a bit like eating chocolate. A few little squares are delicious, satisfying and 'sustainable'. All is good. Gulping down a block or two of chocolate might seem like fun at the time, but the sick feeling you are left with simply makes you feel uncomfortable, sluggish and unhealthy. Do it every day for six months and your health will deteriorate. Such excess is simply is not sustainable. There is, quite obviously, an optimal amount of chocolate one may consume!

It is the same with a strongly growing economy. Steady, solid, but not excessive, growth is good. Sustainability is the key. It would be too much of a good thing if there were to be excessive economic growth for the whole economy achieved via very low interest rates or huge increases in government spending, as this would fuel higher inflation and create a larger budget deficit. That is why the RBA has an inflation target: to prevent higher inflation that would lead to higher interest rates and to slower growth as firms and householders adjusted to a higher interest rate environment.

Economic growth can be too *strong. An 'economic boom', 'bubbles', 'economic overheating' and the consequent labour market 'skills shortages' are all the result of an economy growing too rapidly.*

It simply makes no sense to have all arms of policy set for maximum economic growth.

Economic growth can be *too* strong. An 'economic boom', 'bubbles', 'economic overheating' and the consequent labour market 'skills shortages' are all the result of an economy growing too rapidly. This is exactly why the RBA and government adjust policy levers towards tightening during times of economic strength, so we don't get too much of a good thing.

Apply this principle to your business. When things are very good — too good, in fact — with sales booming and operating costs low, look at the broader economic news. See whether you are just riding this wave of strong economic growth or whether it is a result of something specific that you are doing. Then think about what the policymakers may do if it is an economic boom that is supporting you. Think about the policy changes that might be about to be delivered to slow things down. This is all part of managing your business within the macroeconomy.

Business lending rates

On that note, it is wise to recall that not that long ago, just prior to the GFC, official interest rates were 7.25 per cent and most business borrowing rates were around 11 or 12 per cent. Those high interest rates were a reaction to a jump in inflation, capacity constraints and labour market skills shortages. Fast forward to now and interest rates are hovering at record lows as the RBA reacts to the soft and weak position of the economy and its need for a bit of a pick-me-up (see figure 4.1). The big-picture business cycle matters.

If your business has high gearing and high debt levels but is doing well in a sustained economic upswing, you need to be aware that the business's interest costs will likely rise in the not too distant future. This may well dampen some of that bottom-line improvement in profit that the business was enjoying in the strong growth phase of the cycle. Like a homeowner with a mortgage, a business owner should always have in the back of their mind a financial 'stress test' that looks at the cost of doing business if interest rates are two or even three percentage points higher than today. If it never happens, great. If higher interest rates do eventuate, you have prepared and are likely to cope when this shock comes along.

When interest rates are low, as now, business should focus on other issues that will improve profitability and increase opportunities while keeping a careful eye on debt levels. Debt matters, especially when a business is in expansion mode. Businesses are likely to be accumulating debt to maximise their opportunities as they expand.

Many businesses have changed their focus in recent years in terms of the issues that they judge to be restricting their opportunities to expand and build profits. Recall the various business surveys 10, 15 or 20 years ago? Back then, when businesses were asked to list the main impediments to their business success, 'interest rates' were invariably in the top two or three items mentioned. In today's business surveys interest rates rarely register in the top 10. Now it is red tape, government regulation, the Aussie dollar, tax rates, availability of skilled labour and access to credit that are seen by businesses to be the main impediments to growth.

Things may change. They usually do. Interest rates in the past few years have been remarkably low, but this will not continue indefinitely. Accordingly, it would be wise when managing medium-term business risks to have some form of cash flow contingency that factors in the possibility of interest rates returning to historical averages.

Figure 4.1: Australian business lending rates

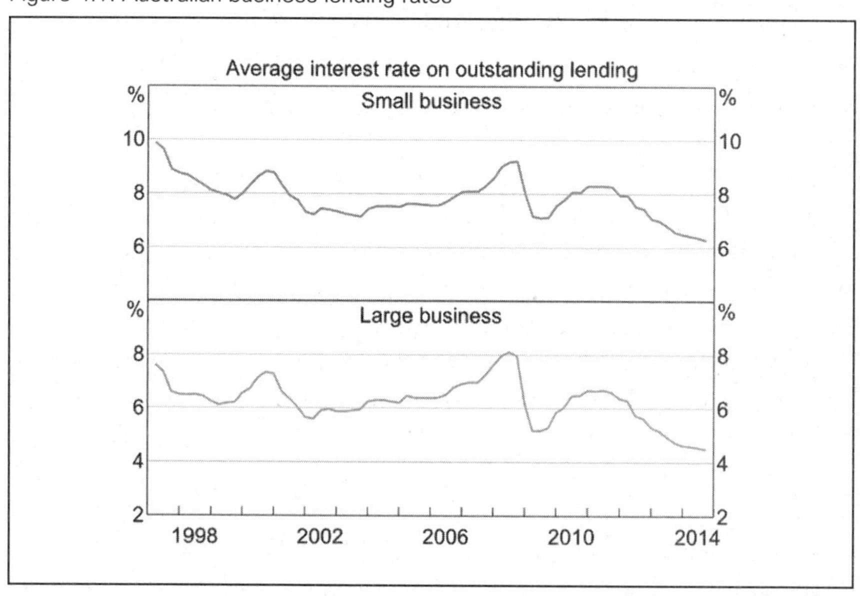

Source: © Australian Prudential Regulation Authority 2015; © Reserve Bank of Australia 2001–2015.

Further implications of big-picture economics

Let's now look at some less obvious ways an economic boom might impact on your business. A strong economy with falling unemployment might mean your business has trouble finding the right workers to allow your firm to develop and expand. One of your competitors may also try to poach your valued and experienced workers by offering a higher wage or better conditions. You may need to match or better that offer or risk losing a crucial asset — your skilled and knowledgeable staff.

For a big-picture macroeconomist, this is good news. It suggests that everyone who wants a job has a job. It is a sign of a flexible labour market and allows the benefits of a strong economy to be shared more equally between the business sector and labour (the workers). This is how a vibrant and dynamic economy should work, with rising incomes and wealth for all resulting from a strong economy. But for you, the business owner looking to retain or hire new staff, it can be a vexing issue that impedes your quest for expansion, growth and higher profitability.

It was not that long ago that the economy was booming and firms had real difficulty finding and then retaining skilled and semi-skilled workers. Pay rates were increased to retain valued staff. It was as simple as that, and as it should be in the sort of flexible labour market environment that Australia currently enjoys.

But what it also means is that your workers may be enticed to leave your business as they hunt for higher paying jobs. Finding a hamburger flipper on low wages can be hard if potential workers have been lured away by the high wages associated with driving trucks or preparing meals in the mining sector. The mining boom and the resulting shortage of workers had major implications not just for the mining sector but for other parts of the economy from which skilled and even semi-skilled workers were drawn away.

Now, as the mining boom turns into a mining bust, the opposite is occurring and wages growth is now very low (see figure 4.2). Indeed, wages growth during 2014 was the lowest ever recorded. This was the highly flexible labour market in Australia doing what it should, with wages adjusting to the business cycle and the change in the unemployment rate.

Figure 4.2: Wage Price Index growth

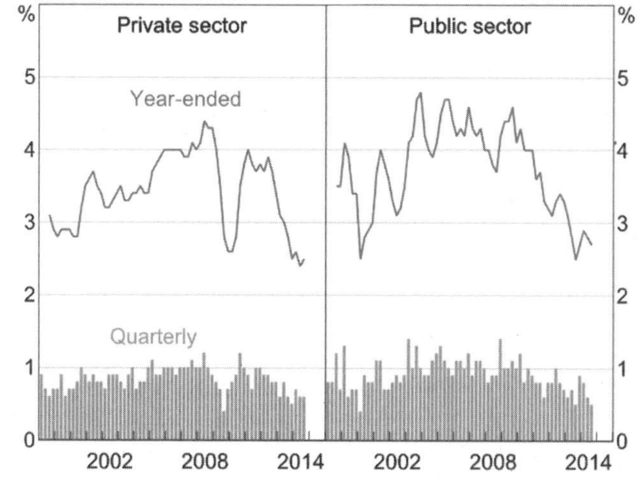

Source: © Australian Bureau of Statistics 2015.

A FLEXIBLE LABOUR MARKET

What is a flexible labour market? These simple illustrations will show how a flexible labour market works.

If the economy is strong and the unemployment rate is falling sharply, the supply of labour drops as demand for labour increases. A flexible labour market would mean rising wages growth in response to the shortage of workers.

When an economy is slowing and the unemployment rate is edging up, the supply of labour rises at the same time as demand for it falls. A flexible labour market leads to falling wages growth.

(continued)

A FLEXIBLE LABOUR MARKET *(cont'd)*

In the period up to early 2008, a booming economy saw the unemployment rate drop to just 4 per cent, the lowest level since the 1970s. Wages growth, in annual terms, rose from around 3 per cent in 2001 to around 4.5 per cent in 2008. This is the textbook reaction to strong ongoing demand for labour.

Since then, as the unemployment rate has risen to around 6.5 per cent, wages growth has slowed to around 2.5 per cent, the lowest ever recorded. Again, this is a textbook example of labour market flexibility.

These facts confirm that Australia has a flexible labour market. In your business you need to be aware that in good times you will have to 'pay up' to obtain and retain good staff, but when things are a little weaker the rate of wage increases should be lower.

Remember that in a flexible labour market and in good economic times, once you find valuable, experienced and reliable staff you need to look after them and build two-way loyalty — you to them and them to you. It will be worth it, probably saving you money in the long run.

Business owners need to be innovative and well prepared. Just because you can't control the big-picture economic trends does not mean you ignore them. Rather, keep in the front of your mind the plans needed to adjust as these trends start to impact on your business. You need to monitor and, where possible, anticipate those changes if your business is to thrive.

Given Australia's economic outlook as outlined for the next one, three and even five years, what should you do when planning for the risks ahead?

Business owners need to be innovative and well prepared. Just because you can't control the big-picture economic trends does not mean you ignore them.

As is always the case, different sectors will experience different growth patterns. Who will win and who will lose? Which states, territories and cities will do well or poorly? Given that we have a clear idea that Australia's terms of trade are now in a long-run decline, it seems fair to assume that governments will be striving to balance the budget and even get to surpluses. Our house price boom is likely to be followed by an extended period of flat and maybe even falling prices. These trends, too, will no doubt impact on your business.

And what of the risk of the Australian dollar moving structurally lower in the years ahead with a move below the long-run average of 75 US cents? What if we see the Aussie dollar around 60 or 65 US cents for a few years? If this happens, online retailing will quickly switch away from overseas purchases and back to local purchases. Local retailers will rejoice, even if it means the price of imported items increases with the lower dollar.

When the Australian dollar was above parity with the US dollar a couple of years ago, a US$100 price tag was, quite plainly, equivalent to AU$100. If, as some people are suggesting, the Aussie dollar weakens to hover at, say, 75 US cents, that US$100 purchase suddenly becomes AU$125. Increasingly, it will be cheaper to buy local. Is your business ready for this?

Is a recession looming?

Another economic cloud hangs over Australia. Statistically speaking, Australia is due for a recession.

The average advanced industrialised country sustains a recession every seven to eight years, on average. Be aware that recessions come around reasonably frequently. Australia, quite spectacularly, has not had a recession for a generation but the odds suggest we will experience one soon.

It is very difficult to accurately forecast the timing of the next recession. Normally, when one appears to be threatening, the RBA cuts interest rates, the Australian dollar falls, the government delivers some fiscal policy stimulus and the recession is avoided. This proactive policy response is a bit like turning the steering wheel to avoid a truck hurtling towards you. Since the last recession in Australia in the early 1990s, all recessionary threats have been headed off in this way. Those include the 1997–98 Asian financial crisis, the 2000–01 US Nasdaq tech wreck and, most famously, the 2008–10 global banking and financial crisis (GFC).

As this book goes to print, there are some vague hints of recessionary elements appearing in Australia. Nevertheless a sober reading suggests there is still a low probability of a recession in the next year or two. Importantly, a negative influence on the economy is the fact that Australia is facing a sharp fall in its terms of trade. The current government seems hell bent on moving the budget to surplus, a policy decision that will act as a handbrake on growth. At the same time, the house price boom that supported household wealth, spending and confidence is cooling. All of this adds to the risk of a recession around the corner.

WHAT IS A RECESSION?

Conventionally, an economic recession is indicated by two consecutive quarters in which real GDP falls. The reality, however, at least from a business perspective, suggests this definition is somewhat artificial and, frankly, a little silly.

'Two negative quarters of GDP growth' takes no account of context — what happens over a slightly longer time frame, or the country in question.

Let me explain it this way.

Think of Australia and let's assume we have the following quarterly real GDP growth rates:

- Quarter 1: –0.5 per cent
- Quarter 2: +0.2 per cent
- Quarter 3: –0.8 per cent
- Quarter 4: +0.3 per cent.

According to the textbook or conventional definition, there is no recession, because in this illustration there have not been two consecutive quarters in which GDP has fallen. But over the course of the four quarters that make up this particular year, GDP has fallen 0.8 per cent. If this occurred in Australia, the unemployment rate would be around two percentage points higher, businesses would be failing and plainly it would be a recession.

Of course, much will also depend on the country you are trying to judge. Take China, for example. It's potential rate of annual GDP growth is widely estimated to be around 7 per cent. That means China's GDP can expand by 7 per cent before there are problems with inflation, capacity utilisation and potential imbalances in the broader economy.

Let's make an assumption that in a particular year China's GDP grew by 4 per cent, or about 1 per cent per quarter. This would be quite catastrophic for the economy. Its banking sector would be in turmoil, deflation risks would abound and for all intents and purposes the country would be in recession. It would simply be growing too slowly.

So, the best definition of recession? It is a tough call to make, but it needs to take account of the extent to which a country's growth drops below its long-run potential, the labour market deteriorates (the unemployment rate rises) and inflation falls below the central bank target.

All businesses need to be aware that the business cycle is always alive and dynamic. Periods of strong growth will pose challenges as you work out what it is best to do. There will also be economic downturns, which will be challenging in a different way. There may even be periods when growth is merely reasonable, being neither strong nor weak.

Over the past couple of years, as I have toured Australia speaking at conferences and business meetings to tens of thousands of people, I have frequently been told, in effect, 'I know we haven't had a recession, but boy, at times it has felt like one'.

No doubt this reflects our multi-speed economy, which by definition has seen some sectors, such as housing, do very well and others, such as manufacturing and the public service, do very poorly. So even if a technical recession is averted, there will be periods and some business sectors where it still might feel like a recession.

Managing your business in a recession

So what can you do to manage your business if a recession does emerge?

Firstly, it may be about managing costs. It may prove harder to encourage customers to come and spend money in your business, especially during an economic downturn, than it is to cut some costs. It should always be the case that your business costs are contained and spending in your business well targeted and productive. In an economic downturn or recession items such as overtime, advertising and some capital expenditure need to be trimmed with extra vigour. Reducing debt levels will also lower interest costs and free up cash flow.

Even in a recession there are business opportunities. More businesses fail in recessions than in good times, certainly, but even in periods of weak growth tens of thousands of businesses start up in Australia every quarter. When GDP falls, the economy still produces goods and services, people still spend money and businesses still invest. It is just at a level that is, in aggregate, weaker than in times of strong economic growth.

In an economic downturn or recession items such as overtime, advertising and some capital expenditure need to be trimmed with extra vigour.

Depending on what sort of business you are in, you can still make money, make a profit or, in a near worst case, get through the tough times so that when the cycle picks up again, which it always does, you will be in a position to return to prosperity.

The critical issues can be boiled down to a range of questions, including which sectors will be strong over the next few years and why, where are the laggards and just how important is Australia's reliance on exports of commodities? China is already more important to us and the world than the US. Being alert to these changing external dynamics has helped Australia prosper and avoid recession for nearly a quarter of a century.

Figure 4.3 shows how Australia's trade patterns have changed over the past 15 years or so. If your business operates in the export space, there may be some lessons in this extraordinary graph.

Figure 4.3: Australian exports by destination

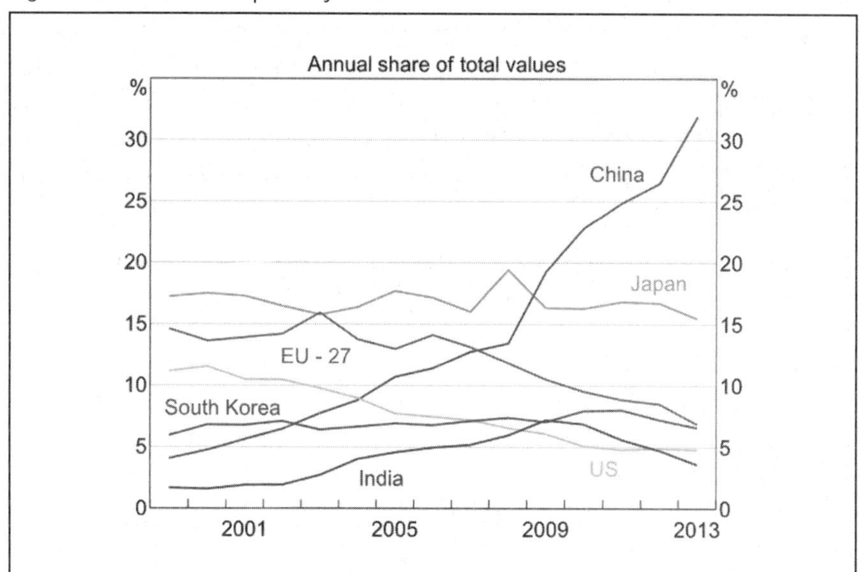

Source: © Australian Bureau of Statistics 2015.

Certainly, the staggering growth in exports to China has focused almost exclusively on natural resources — notably, iron ore and coal — but inbound tourism and education exports to China have also been growing at a rapid pace. Japan, South Korea and India remain very important export destinations and the mantra of the last decade of the 'Asian century' should be apparent.

The long-run decline of Europe and the United States as trading partners for Australia is likely to continue, even though they will remain powerful forces in the world economy and financial markets for many years.

For the domestic economy, which section of the economy will be most dynamic? Will it be retail, housing, construction, transport, banking and finance, mining, aged care, health care, IT, the public service, manufacturing ...? Where to for these sectors?

With an ageing population and compulsory superannuation, health and aged care services should continue to grow. So too will banking, finance and insurance services. Houses will still be built, as will hotels, shopping centres and other infrastructure. Indeed, with the Commonwealth and state governments embarking on an infrastructure spending surge, it is likely that construction and engineering activity will be strong for several more years. But for manufacturing, the public service and even mining, the outlook is less rosy, with structural and other long-run negative factors hindering activities in these areas.

Of course these things can and will change. There are already some early signs that the public service cuts of the past few years have gone too far, with government departments unable to do all of the work allocated to them. The Tax Office, for example, has had staff numbers severely reduced, which has meant that its capacity to chase up tax dodgers and undertake proper audits is severely depleted. A future government may deem it appropriate to rebuild the public services, which of course would benefit the business community in Canberra.

Perhaps the structural adjustments in the economy will take a different course if the lower Australian dollar stays low or falls even further. Will this see niche manufacturing do well? Will there be a tourism and education export boom and the resources required to support it?

While recent trends in the economy have been clear and the short-term outlook is reasonably easy to predict, medium-term trends are subject to many unknowns for your business. This gets to the crux of the advice outlined in this chapter, and indeed the book generally—that is, keep up with the economic and financial market news, and be alert to changes that occur in the economy and policy setting. As you see these trends unfold, adjust your business plan. Be quick to act either to defend your position or to swoop on new opportunities that open up.

As you manage your business, think of the impact of interest rates and work on the assumption that they will not stay low forever; or indeed, when the cycle has turned, they will not stay high forever. Also work on optimising your level of debt. With interest rates now low, consider locking in your borrowing costs for at least a few years. Given how low the borrowing costs now are, there may be no better time to realise that business expansion project you have been putting off because of the debt needed or some other reason. Interest rates matter to borrowers and savers, be they consumers or business owners.

Keep up with the economic and financial market news, and be alert to changes that occur in the economy and policy setting. As you see these trends unfold, adjust your business plan. Be quick to act either to defend your position or to swoop on new opportunities that open up.

So too with the Australian dollar. Will it ever get above parity again? Not that long ago it was under 50 US cents. Could it ever fall that low again? What would it mean to your business if it moves to either of these extremes, or stays near where it currently is?

As a business owner or manager, you have lots of things to consider. Although you cannot control every variable that will affect your business, you need at least to be aware that those uncontrollable issues will impact on your profitability.

KEY POINTS

- The performance of the economy matters to your business, so monitor it closely.
- Economic policies change, so be alert to interest rate risks, tax changes and government spending decisions, all of which may impact on your sales and profits.
- Your staff are your best asset. Good staff are also a potential asset for your competitors, so look after them and build two-way loyalty.
- Australia has not experienced a recession for a quarter of a century. The odds favour one soon, but the RBA and government are likely to take protective measures if the threat of one escalates.
- Australia's economic future is inexorably tied up with Asia — look for business and investment opportunities there if you can.

chapter five
YOUR SUPERANNUATION

As a worker and then a retiree, you should recognise superannuation as a paramount issue. Saving money throughout your career via superannuation will provide you with a decent nest-egg later, when you retire. Making contributions over and above the compulsory employer payments yields terrific benefits, especially given the very favourable tax treatment that, for the moment, still applies.

It is difficult to convince a young person that chipping in even a few extra dollars a year will benefit them significantly when they retire. I suppose that is fair enough given the temptations of the young to spend their scarce money now, doing nice things—going out, having fun.

Which is one reason why superannuation is compulsory. For many young people, paying back their university debt or scrounging for a deposit on that elusive first home takes priority over superannuation. But a little extra superannuation savings early on can yield a terrific long-run return.

The fact that superannuation is compulsory means that every worker has some money flowing into their retirement income from the time they start working, perhaps as a teenager. So everyone *should* be interested in where their money is invested and how much they are accruing.

Let's start with some basics.

The purpose of the government superannuation scheme

When you get a job, your employer is required by law to pay a contribution to your superannuation fund. Whether you are earning big dollars or very little, from your very first job you will start building a retirement nest-egg. That is something to be celebrated — it is money that is yours, with the important condition that you cannot touch it until you are aged between 60 and 70 depending on your year of birth. In other words, only when you have retired can you get your hands on that money and use it. This was the objective of the scheme when it was established in the early 1990s — it was aimed at building, for everyone, a decent retirement income at a level above the public pension. There was the added benefit of saving future governments a fortune in age pensions and, in turn, freeing up funds to cover other aspects of an ageing population such as aged care and health services. It also built domestic savings levels and has seen huge investment opportunities for superannuation fund managers.

Your funds are building with each payday contribution and with ongoing investment returns, so even on low balances in the early years you need to be alert to how this money is being put to work.

Those who start working at age 20 and continue through to 65, for example, will see 45 years of compulsory contributions accrue in their superannuation fund. Even with moderate rates of return of, say, 6 per cent per annum this will build to a decent amount of money for them to enjoy in their retirement years.

The size of this investment of your money for retirement should encourage you to pay very close attention to how and where the funds are invested and the fees you pay each year. Your funds are building with each payday contribution and with ongoing investment returns, so even on low balances in the early years you need to be alert to how this money is being put to work. As you approach retirement, you need to position the fund to preserve it, reducing the investment risk but still ensuring a decent rate of return. I will touch on these issues a little later in the chapter.

You can't afford not to pay attention!

In the middle of 2014 polling company Essential Research conducted a poll of around 1000 people in which respondents were asked a series of questions relating to their superannuation. For anyone interested in the big-picture benefits to individuals from having and managing superannuation, the results were frightening. The survey showed that only 15 per cent of people paid 'a lot of attention ... to the arrangements for your retirement income, such as your superannuation returns, and fees, wealth management and other forms of long term savings'.

A lousy 15 per cent, or just one in seven people!

The survey found that an additional 33 per cent 'paid some attention', 29 per cent 'not much attention', 16 per cent 'no attention' and 7 per cent 'don't know' when it came to these crucial arrangements for their retirement income.

These are shocking and painful findings. Painful because they show that over half the population have no interest or no idea how their retirement savings are being looked after, how or whether they are growing and, almost by definition, whether they will have enough money to live on when they retire.

I hope you are not one of them.

These findings were matched by results from a survey conducted by REST, a large superannuation fund, which revealed that of those aged 50 years and over, a staggering 35 per cent were 'completely unprepared' for retirement, with just 14 per cent 'financially prepared'. The other 50-odd per cent were only partially prepared for retirement.

With this level of indifference to how their own money is being managed and how poorly they are setting themselves up for retirement, it is little wonder there are people unknowingly subjected to high fees and shonky practices. Those with little or no interest in their superannuation are easy targets for those dodgy operators in the funds management industry who give the rest of the industry a bad name.

The obvious rhetorical question is, how do you know you are being ripped off if you pay no attention and don't know anything about your superannuation savings?

I suspect this disengagement is also why so many people, as they approach retirement, bemoan the fact that they do not have enough money in their fund. Well, to be blunt, they should have been paying attention and tracking what was happening to their super funds throughout their work life. The Essential Research poll found that of those aged 55 and over, a combined total of 33 per cent were in the categories of 'not much attention', 'no attention' or 'don't know' when it came to their retirement money. So even among the oldies one-third of those in or approaching retirement had no idea about their superannuation.

Even more disconcerting, the survey asked the straightforward but critically important question, 'Do you know how much you are paying in fees each year to your superannuation fund?' And just 18 per cent of respondents claimed to 'know exactly' how much their fees were.

Slightly more encouragingly, a further 41 per cent said they knew 'approximately' how much their fees were. Of course, this means that a staggeringly high 40 per cent did not know how much they were paying for the management of their superannuation fund and their money, even though those annual fees can amount to many hundreds, even thousands, of dollars.

I wonder how many of these people know (and then complain about) the price of electricity? Or petrol? Or their caffe latte? Or bananas when a cyclone hits Queensland?

Superannuation fees vary widely from fund to fund so, as in all aspects of life when it comes to spending your money, it pays to shop around. The level of superannuation fees paid has a huge bearing on the size of your nest-egg when you do retire. Like compound interest, paying fees that are even 0.5 per cent per annum lower over the decades your superannuation fund exists can mean the difference between a comfortable retirement and one defined by financial pressures.

The Essential Research poll did offer the small comfort that only 19 per cent of those aged 55 and over had no idea of the fees they paid, with 81 per cent having at least some idea of their fees. This suggests that in most cases the older you get, the more attention you pay to the fees you are paying.

And the more money you have in superannuation, the greater are the fees you pay, which makes it even more important to lower your fees at all times, but especially as you get closer to retirement and your fund grows.

But imagine anyone, even youngsters, not knowing where and how much of their money they are spending? In part this is because the fees are deducted from your superannuation account each quarter or year, rather than directly from your bank account, credit card or wallet. As a result, most people don't know and seemingly don't care about these post-fee. They just look at the fees return and the balance outstanding, or so it seems.

On a superannuation balance of $100 000, a 0.5 per cent *difference* in the fees you are charged is worth a cool $500 a year. And the more money you have in superannuation, the greater are the fees you pay, which makes it even more important to lower your fees at all times, but especially as you get closer to retirement and your fund grows. Compound that amount over a couple of decades and you can see why even a seemingly small difference in the level of fees can lead to a difference of $50 000 or $100 000 in your final retirement nest-egg. And this is just the fees, not the return or yield on your contributions.

Life-cycle investment

Clearly, it pays to position your fund with the best (most favourable to you) fee structure. If you don't have a lot of time to manage your fund, it might be wise to go for a low-risk or balanced investment strategy. After you sort out the fee level for your superannuation account, you need to reflect on how old you are, because choosing which asset class or financial instruments you want to invest in should be carefully linked to your age.

I hesitate to remind you of this self-evident fact, but the older you are, the closer you are to the end of your life. In other words, you may be running out of time for your superannuation to bounce back from a high-risk, high-return investment strategy should a market crash come along (which they do all too frequently). A young person with a high-risk, high-return investment strategy can wait three or five or even more years for their investment strategy to bounce back from a crash, whereas someone in their seventies or older who also needs the money to live off may not have that luxury; they may need to sell their assets to live off at the depths of a market decline.

The importance of this life-cycle investment strategy, or rather the fact that many people did not have such a strategy, was plainly exposed in the recent market turmoil during the global financial crisis.

When the value of the Australian share market dropped by around 50 per cent in the wake of the GFC, those investors whose portfolios had a high weighting towards stocks (rather than bonds or term deposits) lost a lot of cash. Many who had been poorly advised were already retired, in their mid to late seventies, and did not have the opportunity to watch the market bounce back and to recoup their losses.

The net value of their superannuation funds was effectively halved. Yields from many superannuation funds were slashed and income from whatever funds were in term deposits got crunched as interest rates were slashed from 7 or 8 per cent down to 3 or 4 per cent.

Consider the scenario of a well-off retiree with $1 million in superannuation before the GFC. Assuming an 80 per cent weighting in stocks with an average dividend yield of 4 per cent, and 20 per cent in term deposits, earning 8 per cent. The income from this balance would be a little below $50 000 per year.

This type of portfolio for someone aged, say, 75 years or more who is already retired, and without the benefit of a long time to allow share markets to recover, is dreadful. It ignores one of the most basic objectives in managing retirement money — life-cycle investment.

In the immediate aftermath of the GFC, this investor would have their holdings reduced to $600 000, with just $400 000 in stocks and $200 000 still in term deposits when the dust settled.

Resetting the portfolio to work out the income flow for the year ahead with these new balances, a steady dividend yield of 4 per cent, and 4 per cent on the term deposits to reflect the lower interest rate environment, slashes the annual return to under $25 000. This reflects a massive loss of income as well as a huge chunk of capital destroyed. Less wealth, less income.

Had this retiree had a more sensible and prudent investment balance ahead of the GFC, say with 80 per cent in term deposits and 20 per cent in shares, these holdings would have fallen only marginally, to $900 000. The annual income would have still reduced but would have held above $35 000, which was more to do with lower interest rates than wealth destruction. Indeed, it would be possible to draw down on the capital in the fund if needed and still be a long way ahead.

Life-cycle investment is critical. Your age is one vital determinant of what sort of financial risks you should be taking for your retirement income.

This simple example provides a stark but valuable lesson on managing your superannuation, especially as you get older. It illustrates all too clearly a general lack of awareness of how to manage your investments according to your age. Life-cycle investment is critical. Your age is one vital determinant of what sort of financial risks you should be taking for your retirement income.

Young people who quite rightly choose to invest in a high-risk, high-return growth fund probably should not worry unduly if their superannuation investment goes down sharply from time to time because of an economic or market ruction. This is because in time the market will almost inevitably recover. At some stage it will have a fantastic bounce to restore and then add to the value of the investment fund. Young people have years, if not decades, to see a market rebound and a lift after a market slump. And while they are waiting, they are also adding to the funds as they work.

The older you are, the less you should invest in high-risk assets, and the more conservative your investment strategy needs to be.

People in later life cannot afford to have too much invested in high-risk investments. Your retirement will be miserable if your investment portfolio has a heavy bias in favour of stocks and there is a stock market rout a few years after you stop working. The message of life-cycle investing is simple: the older you are, the less you should invest in high-risk assets, and the more conservative your investment strategy needs to be. The older you are, the more you should be investing in things like term deposits and bonds. Boring, but safe.

Of course, that means you will not enjoy that time when the market, for whatever reasons, jumps 40 or 50 per cent or more over a few years, but nor will you suffer an erosion of assets when a market slump occurs. I suspect that if they had known more about how their superannuation money was being managed, most 75-year-olds in the lead into the GFC would have been more than happy to preserve their capital and been content with a low investment return, even if it meant missing out on the possibility of a stellar return.

All this means you need to think about where you have your money now. If you are over 60, think about starting to pare back risky investments and tilt towards safe, low-yield investments. It will be unexciting but you will, at the very least, preserve all (yes, all) of the capital that is invested in term deposits and government bonds.

Emerging policy changes

There are a few emerging policy matters that are important for you and your superannuation.

The government has indicated that the retirement age will increase to 70 years by 2035. This reflects an increase in life expectancy, and from the government's perspective it is a long-run change designed to lower government spending on age pensions and improve the structural position of the budget over the long term. It is also designed to increase workforce participation. Older people staying in the workforce will add to economic growth, contributing income tax while funding their own lifestyle.

If you are currently under the age of 40, this will mean you have to work longer before getting access to the pension, or indeed to your super money, but it also mean you will have an extra five years of paid employment to contribute to superannuation.

One issue with the lifting of the retirement age to 70 is the question of whether or not there will be the right sorts of jobs available for older workers. Physically demanding jobs, such as in trades or personal training or professional sports, will be among many occupation types that are unlikely to be filled by those aged 65 to 70. On the other hand, if the current trend towards services jobs continues, it is likely that by 2035 these jobs will be ones that an older person can comfortably do.

Older people staying in the workforce will add to economic growth, contributing income tax while funding their own lifestyle.

The increase in the retirement age could be good news for people wanting to build their superannuation savings, with the five extra years of paid work and super contributions. The reality, however, might be quite different given that many people already opt to retire early, before they reach the age of 65. This may reflect of some of the earlier strategies mentioned, such as downsizing and using the extra cash to live on before being allowed to access superannuation savings.

Either way, it is just another change, again linked to your age, that you should feed into your retirement planning.

How much will you need?

How much do you need to accumulate in your superannuation for a comfortable retirement?

Of course that depends on many factors. In today's dollar terms, let's say a couple needs around $40 000 a year to cover food, rates, insurance, health costs, ad hoc unexpected expenses (that hot-water system blows up!), gardening, utilities bills and a bit of fun, whatever that may mean for you. This assumes you own your house and are not paying rent or the mortgage (as discussed in earlier chapters).

Some would suggest $40 000 a year is too generous, as it is well above the pension rate. Others may say it is a bit low if you want to include overseas travel and other high-cost expenses. My aim is to frame the issues you need to think about so you can avoid relying on the age pension and thereby have even more money for a more comfortable retirement. I'll use the example of $40 000 to illustrate the factors to consider when you are planning and saving for your retirement, but these calculations can be tweaked to suit your particular circumstances.

Let's work on what looks to be a pretty generous assumption that over the next few decades the return on your superannuation fund is likely to average 5 per cent.

Structurally low interest rates and dividends will be helped along a bit by capital gains via productivity growth and innovation, but 5 per cent seems about right, on average, over a long time frame for a balanced portfolio in an environment of very low inflation and demographic trends likely to impact unfavourably on future GDP growth.

To achieve a $40 000 return, you will need around $800 000 in your superannuation fund in today's dollar terms. If we assume 6 per cent return, you still need to accumulate $675 000. At 4 per cent, you need $1 million. This is quite obviously a substantial amount of money and well above the average superannuation balance currently held by most Australians (remember, I am talking about the combined funds of a couple now).

It is a relatively large amount and a multiple of most people's current superannuation savings for several reasons. Importantly, the compulsory component of superannuation has been in place for less than 25 years. This has not allowed everyone in the workforce, especially those close to retirement, sufficient time to build a large pool of savings. Working for around 45 years under this regime can be expected to lift the average balance substantially over the next 20 years. Many of those people who were, for example, 45 years old when superannuation was made compulsory in the early 1990s started their retirement savings with a near-zero balance and completed about half their working lives with no accumulated retirement income savings. This will change for younger Australians with each successive year of superannuation contributions and with the benefit of cumulative market returns.

Another reason for the shortfall in current superannuation balances is that the currently prescribed minimum of 9.5 per cent superannuation contributions is simply not enough to get the level of funds sufficiently high to deliver an adequate nest-egg, even after 45 years of working.

This is why, at various stages in the development of superannuation policy since the early 1990s, compulsory superannuation contribution legislation has had targets of 12 per cent or even 15 per cent of wages to be paid into your retirement income account. Unfortunately for those looking to build a decent retirement income pool, or indeed for future generations of taxpayers, political expediency has seen progress towards these targets cut or frozen, with the current government pushing back the timetable for higher contributions for half a decade. Under the current government's law, superannuation contributions will reach only 10 per cent of income in 2021–22 and 12 per cent in 2025–26. This will help someone born in 2005 to retire in 2075, but you can see why so many people still fall short of what is a desirable pool of savings.

It is clear that you need to take the matter of your retirement security into your own hands, because the current 9.5 per cent current rate of contributions will not be quite sufficient for you.

Simply put, the long-run objective of having a greater proportion of the population self-sufficient in their retirement will be thwarted and the call on the public purse via the budget will be greater in 10, 20 and 30 years' time because of the political decision to postpone higher contributions.

It is clear that you need to take the matter of your retirement security into your own hands, because the current 9.5 per cent current rate of contributions will not be quite sufficient for you. The still favourable tax treatment of superannuation makes it all the more attractive, and even necessary, to make some so-called salary sacrifice or other voluntary contributions to the fund now to boost your retirement income.

As reiterated throughout this book, the key point is to be aware of all of these and other issues that impact on your finances. Pay attention to what is happening to your money. In the case of superannuation, you have a huge incentive to do that—it is your savings, your money and your retirement you are managing. And you should do so right from the time you start working and contributing to a super scheme.

Let's assume for a moment that instead of the money being locked away in superannuation, your retirement income sat in your day-to-day bank account. You would no doubt watch it closely and be aware of when money was going in, when it was being drawn down and what fees you were paying to the bank to manage the account. You would shop around for the best interest rate and lowest fee combination, and you would change financial institutions if you could get a better deal. You would notice in an instant if there was an error in the account or any other anomalies. You also wouldn't entrust your savings to someone you have never met or with whom you have only a cursory relationship. You need to apply the degree of diligence you exercise with your day-to-day banking to your superannuation money too.

Self-managed superannuation funds

A concern for due diligence and a lack of trust in some fund managers are the main reasons why self-managed superannuation funds are so popular and have been growing so strongly in recent years.

Self-managed superannuation funds attract those with a high level of interest in and knowledge of their personal finances. When you run your own super fund, you write the cheques (or make the transfers) that pay for its operation and you tend to be careful to minimise and control these costs, which might otherwise eat into your savings.

You also know exactly where your money is being invested — the risks you are taking by holding shares in a speculative mining company, for example, versus a term deposit with one of the solid local banks. You know when interest and dividend payments are due to flow into your account, and you have only yourself to blame when things go wrong. And when they go right!

With a self-managed fund, *you* are the fund manager, but without the overheads of a plush office, advertising and other costs that commercial fund managers have, and those economies are obviously passed on to you. Once your savings reach a critical mass, it is usually cheaper to run your own fund than having your money managed by a commercial fund manager.

The lower financial cost of running your superannuation comes at a different cost: it takes some time, some work and some reading to maintain your fund. The benefits of this effort should be weighed against the probability that you would be paying higher fees and have less control over your own retirement savings if they were with a professional manager.

As noted, there is also the issue of how financially savvy you are when it comes to running your fund. You can still throw away a lot of money by holding some of the high-fee exchange-traded funds, trading too frequently, falling for the lure of the latest stock tips, having your broker peddle the latest offering or investing in that property trust that you realise too late ties your money up for a decade. As the manager of your self-managed fund, you must be prepared to spend a good deal of time looking after your money, learning about markets and knowing what to look out for.

Suffice to say, looking after your retirement income in your own self-managed superannuation fund has much merit, but given the complexity of many financial instruments and investments, and the time you need to invest to do it well, it is not for everyone.

Other superannuation opportunities

There are a few other issues with superannuation that are worth considering.

Investment opportunities are global, not just limited to Australia. Money can be invested in Chinese stocks, emerging market bonds, US housing, European manufacturing companies, African agriculture—the list is almost endless. These investments are not for the faint hearted. As soon as you place funds overseas you take on an extra element of risk, with currency fluctuations impacting on your return in Australian dollars.

For those with an appetite for these sorts of investments, the fees tend to be higher than simply taking out term deposits or buying a few ASX-listed stocks, but the diversification and opportunities are sometimes worth considering. Don't forget there can be some messy tax issues with foreign-earned income, so tread carefully if you wish to invest in this area.

In summary, your superannuation money needs to be managed and monitored to help you achieve your objective of building up a pool of money sufficient to fund a comfortable retirement.

KEY POINTS

- Know where you superannuation money is, the fees you are paying and where the investments are being made.
- Start early in your working life. If possible, add a few dollars to the compulsory contributions each payday.
- As you get older and closer to retirement, assess the balance of your investments and choose the less risky assets.
- Self-managed superannuation funds suit some people. You know where the money is and your running costs, but it takes some time and knowledge to do it properly.
- IT IS YOUR MONEY — LOOK AFTER IT!

chapter six

YOUR GOVERNMENT

Whichever side of politics is in government, you can be sure that the push to tighter budget policy will continue for the next few years and maybe even well into the 2020s. There is a general acceptance that moving towards a balanced budget and then a budget surplus within the next few years is desirable, provided the economy is strong enough to withstand a lift in taxes or a drop in spending.

This means that when you are framing your personal finances or business plans, you should expect your government to lean towards higher taxes and increased costs for services (at the time of writing Medicare payments and university fees are a couple of hotly debated current issues). At the same time, look for further cuts to government services. Governments, both Coalition and Labor, want to move to budget surpluses, which by definition means they will have to collect more revenue from taxpayers than they will spend on services, infrastructure and transfers.

Microeconomic policy options

Other policy issues important for the economy, such as industrial relations, climate change, skills training, the environment, education, ageing and industry policy, will be debated, tinkered with and in some cases reformed. These areas of microeconomic policy are less about the budget than about trying to make the Australian economy more efficient and productive. Which way the policy action swings in these areas depends largely on who is in government. But it is safe to say that they will remain dominant issues for government, and that they are vitally important both in themselves and to complement policies aimed at the budget bottom line.

One policy issue that never seems to go away is tax. Who knows which way tax reform will go, and not just in the next year or two. Over the next decade, the government could well look to boost revenue through a higher and broader goods and services tax, higher petrol taxes, and less generous tax treatment for negative gearing and superannuation, for example. As for what might be good ideas for tax reform — that is, changes that are fair and economically efficient — there is also the challenge of having those changes pass the Parliament.

Politics is likely to remain ugly. This means it will be easier to oppose than to propose major economic policy reforms. It also means that the delivery of any reforms or significant policy changes will likely be slow and cumbersome as political negotiations unfold and drag on. Contributing difficulties include an inevitably hostile Senate not just now but seemingly forever with a range of erratic minor parties and Independents determining what policy changes go through. Inevitably, there will have to be compromise with the minor parties to pass the more significant policy changes. This will probably translate into a lack of zeal for reform on the part of the government. Political realities point to a greater risk that something will go wrong within the economy while our government dithers on the policy changes that need to be made.

Most politicians of all colours know what the right policies are, but politically they are too hard to implement.

There is likely to be very little in the way of bipartisan support for economic policy reform. This means questions of tax reform, industrial relations, spending cuts and changes to charges for government services will be hotly contested. In their heart of hearts, most politicians of all colours know what the right policies are, but politically they are too hard to implement. They are sure to offend one of their key constituencies, and in any case it is easier to oppose a policy than to work hard to win popular support for it.

Consequently, there are a couple of risks that will emerge from your government — risks that will result from shying away from some short-term political pain even though the reforms would help set Australia up for a decade or so of growth. I hope I am wrong, but necessary reforms are likely to be watered down or avoided altogether, which will mean a less than ideal structure for the economy. We could be about to see a long period of dithering and piecemeal work on policy changes, a muddle-through approach that would be a continuation of what we have been experiencing for years on tax policy and government spending priorities.

All this will impact on the economy and therefore on your financial position.

What will make this policy lethargy all the more problematic for Australia over the next few years is that the rest of the world's economies, particularly Australia's major trading partners in Asia, are growing and expanding at a rapid pace. They are doing this largely via huge investment in education, massive infrastructure development, rising health standards and, to be frank, all the things any decent government in Australia should be pursuing with vigour.

Asia is rapidly catching up and in some instances overtaking Australia in education, skills and living standards. Unless our policy settings are adjusted now, this momentum will see Australia drop a few rungs over the medium term.

'If this is so obvious,' I hear many exclaiming, 'what economic policies are there that could help set Australia up for the next decade but that our politicians are too scared to implement? And why don't they simply do it?'

Asia is rapidly catching up and in some instances overtaking Australia in education, skills and living standards.

In looking at the answers to these questions, it is important to note that a critical aspect of the budget since the GFC, and one likely to prevail for many years to come, is a structural softness in government revenue, especially from tax. The GFC and its hangover have meant that low inflation, low wages and weak capital gains have been the order of the day. This trifecta of economic fundamentals means that government revenue growth has been generally weak, with the low inflation climate all but certain to continue for several years. This underscores the difficulty for your government as it strives to get the revenue it needs to return to surplus and cover the cost of the policy agenda it wishes to pursue.

At one level, low inflation hurts government revenue from the goods and services tax.

Think about this stylised example: A basket of goods and services cost $100.00 and $10.00 GST was paid. The following year, in a higher inflation environment, say of 3 per cent, $103.00 was spent and $10.30 GST was paid to the government. In a slightly lower inflation environment, say of 2 per cent, only $102.00 would be spent on that given basket of goods and services and the GST collection would be just $10.20. It doesn't sound like a big difference when expressed that way; 10 cents per $100.00 of spending seems small but given that in 2013–14, $54 billion of GST was paid, each percentage point on inflation is worth over $500 million in 'lost' or 'extra' tax. The critical issue is that low inflation means the price level on which GST is paid in future years is also lower so the lower tax revenue for the government compounds in future years, especially if inflation stays low.

Then there is the lower growth in personal income tax receipts for the government in a low wage environment. When wages growth is low, the shortfall in revenue for your government is calculated in the same way as in the previous GST example, but from the base of aggregate wages, not spending. Let's say wages growth, which was 4 per cent per annum, slows to growth of just 2.5 per cent. According to the Budget papers, for the PAYG tax base, this 1.5 percentage point difference is worth around $1.5 billion a year in terms of lower income tax payments. And because the lower level of wages cascades out into the future years of the forward estimates, slower wages growth hurts revenue in the budget on a permanent basis, or at least until annual wages growth lifts above 4 per cent.

With the government forecasting that the unemployment rate will hit 6.5 per cent and stay above 6 per cent for a few more years, it seems highly likely that wages growth will be nearer 3 per cent or less, rather than the 4 per cent or more that would apply when the economy is firing on all cylinders.

Weaker growth is a sign of a weaker economy, which in turn makes the task of balancing the budget all the harder.

Which is why, from the position of the budget, let alone the economy and the unemployment rate, your government would be hoping that inflation does not fall below the middle of the RBA's target for 2 to 3 per cent for too long, and that wages do not remain at record lows for too long. Weaker growth is a sign of a weaker economy, which in turn makes the task of balancing the budget all the harder.

Consider too the issue of capital gains tax, given that many asset prices in inflation-adjusted terms are still below the levels of 2007 and 2008. The ASX peaked in late 2007 and while there has been a decent rebound from the GFC lows, it remains well below that pre-GFC high. Add to that the carry forward of capital losses that were particularly acute during the GFC and it is easy to see why government revenue from capital gains taxes remains in the doldrums.

The issue, as you can no doubt see, is that if the government wants to get the budget back to surplus and maintain its level of spending, tax levels have to rise. There are many ways your government can do this. It could very simply increase income taxes, as the Abbott government has done by targeting high-income earners with a 2 per cent levy, or it could simply hike other income taxes in the lower tax brackets. It could, as we have discussed, lift the rate and broaden the base for GST collections, or raise the excise on petrol, tobacco or alcohol. Or there could be a policy change that restricts income tax deductions on items such as negative gearing and superannuation. It could even hike company tax across the board, rather than just for big business as this government has proposed to do when it was looking for ways to help fund its paid parental leave scheme.

Government spending pressures

Some readers will no doubt get carried away by the notion that a budget surplus depends on higher tax receipts and insist, 'It's government spending that should be cut'.

Certainly, there is always a case for keeping a tight rein on government spending within the bounds of the business cycle. In this case growth in government spending can and should rise when the private sector segment of the economy is weak, and it can and should be cut when the economy is strong.

The data on spending show that the issue of returning the budget to balance or even to surplus is related only marginally to government spending. As a share of the economy, government spending is only a little bigger now than in the 1980s, 1990s and 2000s, notwithstanding the recent spending spree by the current government.

One problem with recent governments has been a tendency to make the tough decisions on spending cuts but then to spend the savings elsewhere in the economy.

Government spending, as a share of the economy (GDP, in other words), has swung up and down with the business cycle over the past four decades, but on average it has generally stuck around 25 per cent.

Any money saved by trimming spending as part of the strategy to balance the budget must not simply be channelled back into another area of government expenditure. One problem with recent governments has been a tendency to make the tough decisions on spending cuts but then to spend the savings elsewhere in the economy. The Abbott government has done this spectacularly. Now, the weaker economy means that the overall benefit to the budget bottom line is negative, with projected budget deficits over coming years much larger than those left by the previous government. Moreover the return to budget surplus has been pushed out by five years relative to the projections of the previous government.

JUST HOW BIG IS YOUR GOVERNMENT?

According to recent budget documents, in the 2015–16 financial year total Commonwealth government spending will be around $430 billion while total revenue will be just over $400 billion. Hence the $30 billion deficit.

Of that $400 billion in revenue, just over $375 billion will be in the form of tax receipts with the lion's share coming from income tax, company tax, and the goods and services tax. The other $25 billion of revenue includes receipts from government-owned operating activities including dividends. Recall that in that year Australian GDP will be around $1.7 trillion.

Some might say it should be easy to trim a few per cent from that spending and add a few per cent to revenue from tax changes — and suddenly the budget is back in surplus. And this is true, speaking as an economist.

But politically, the difficulties of implementing policies that stop giving money to people or that collect more tax from them are all too often unpalatable.

By way of reference — and this is always a fun issue to consider — back in 1972–73 total government spending for the year was just $9.3 billion while total government revenue was $9.7 billion. There was a $400 million budget surplus. In the space of a little over 40 years, the size of government has increased more than 40-fold. For those interested, GDP has increased by a little more than 30-fold over the same time frame, so government has become much bigger.

All of this comes back to the issue at hand — tax.

Tax revenues

In the coming years your government will be looking to lift the tax it collects as it works to balance the budget. Both sides of politics will be looking to the revenue or tax side as the main factor to help return the budget to balance and then surplus.

It will also do this because all of us, collectively at least, want the government to provide us with a range of services and protections that any decent, well-off country should insist upon.

The population wants and expects the government to provide things like national security, which is expensive, as is a high-quality health system that is readily accessible for everyone who gets sick. Australians want a decent level of age pension, disability care, good roads and a proper safety net for those who fall on hard times through unemployment. Education spending is a social issue as well as an economic policy. Everyone should have the opportunity to maximise their potential through skills and training.

Yet unless the level of support in these areas is reduced, or indeed the programs currently funded by the government are cut, it will be revenue (tax) that must be lifted if the budget is ever to get to surplus.

Education spending is a social issue as well as an economic policy. Everyone should have the opportunity to maximise their potential through skills and training.

Those who advocate that the government sector should markedly limit their involvement in these areas are generally out of touch with community attitudes, which invariably demand decent service delivery from the government. That said, there are some economic zealots who exercise a powerful influence on the policy and political debate. This was demonstrated by the ill-fated Commission of Audit in 2014, which advocated a range of extreme economic policy changes very similar to the US Tea Party platform. Thankfully the ideas, if they can be called that, were easily discredited on both rational and economic grounds.

The Commission of Audit's recommendations included wage cuts to boost employment, 15 000 job cuts in the public service, a $15 Medicare levy on every visit to the doctor, cuts to funding for the Disability Insurance Scheme and abolition of unemployment payments to people under 30. The recommendations were seen to be unfair, unnecessary and curiously inconsistent with a strong economy and a relatively rich society.

Some spending cuts, paradoxically, end up costing the government money. The decision to slash the number of people working in the Tax Office means the auditing of taxpayers, both corporate and individual, will be compromised and potential tax revenue will be lost. Those advocating smaller government at any cost need to be careful what they wish for.

Some spending cuts, paradoxically, end up costing the government money.

Of course the influence of your government extends well beyond these so-called fiscal measures of government taxation and spending.

Other regulatory issues

Other areas of government policy influence cover a host of matters, often with dual or overlapping responsibilities with state governments. These largely regulatory elements generally cover a range of social policies, from what is taught in schools, and campaigns to reduce smoking, littering, drink driving and obesity, to infrastructure requirements, the environment, Indigenous wellbeing, culture, sport, tourism among many other areas.

If your business or personal finances are linked in any way to these matters, be alert! Regulatory changes on the environment or smoking or tourism, to name a few, can have a serious impact on your financial wellbeing.

One of the better case studies on how your government can influence sectors in the real economy relates to tobacco regulation. Tobacco companies, including those involved in the growing or distribution of tobacco, have a business plan that aims to persuade more people to smoke more cigarettes. Like any other business, they have a profit motive and therefore they lobby the government hard not to do anything that might impinge on their profits or even to change the laws to encourage more people to smoke. This is why the tobacco companies have undertaken such a ferocious campaign against higher taxes on cigarettes, plain packaging laws, advertising bans and health awareness programs. The fewer people who smoke, the fewer sales they make and the lower their potential for profit. Government policies that discourage people from smoking will hurt profits.

GOVERNMENT REGULATION AND SMOKING

One quite stunning aspect of government regulation over several decades has been the spectacular decline in the consumption of tobacco. Since scientific studies proved the link between smoking and premature death, smoking rates have plummeted, and this trend has been assisted by unrelenting and aggressive government policies.

Here are a few stark facts on the decline in tobacco consumption.

According to official data from the Australian Bureau of Statistics, during 2014 the volume of tobacco consumed fell to a record low. Compared with the peak level of tobacco consumption in the mid 1970s, the decline has been just under 60 per cent. Over these 40 years, Australia's population has increased by around 70 per cent. This suggests that the volume of tobacco consumed per capita has fallen by nearly 80 per cent. This is a staggering drop!

The facts that have driven this massive decline include the price of tobacco products, which has increased by around 4000 per cent (yes, 4000 per cent!) over that time largely as a result of a huge increase in excise, the impact of the government ban on tobacco advertising, health warnings on packets, government-funded anti-smoking advertising campaigns and plain packaging regulations.

Data from the ABS and Department of Health show that the proportion of the population who smoke each day fell from 34 per cent in the mid 1980s to 17 per cent in 2011–12.

By any measure, on this issue your government has implemented policies that have worked—and the health of Australians is all the better for it.

If you are in the tobacco business, this is bad news for your turnover and budget bottom line. For the tobacco growers, manufacturers, marketers and retailers, your government has implemented policies that are killing their business. Tough luck, most people would say, because they are doing it for good reason—keeping people alive, improving public health and, importantly, reducing the government's expenditure on health care, given that tens of thousands of people still get sick and die from smoking-related illnesses each year. Less illness equals less government expenditure on health care.

If you are in a business that involves tobacco, you would have seen this coming. And you should expect more of it.

The same argument and line of thinking can be applied to panelbeaters and car parts suppliers. While not as well organised, well funded or vocal as the tobacco lobby, I suspect they hate your government building better roads, installing speed cameras, instituting random breath tests and increasing police monitoring of the roads for dangerous driving. The decline in the number of road accidents that results from your government 'imposing' these changes on you surely means less business related to car repairs.

The impact on you and your business

Can you see where I am coming from with these examples?

Government regulations, and not just its taxing and spending decisions, can influence your business. As all of these decisions impact on you and your finances, it pays to know what the government is doing and planning to do. You can then take steps to adjust your business accordingly.

Note that many government policies are not just good for business, they are *great*. Being in construction during an infrastructure boom, having an aged care or childcare business when government money is being directed to these areas are a couple of positive examples. More spending on education raises the skill level of workers available for your business. Potential workers can read, write, add up, think, innovate, sell, drive, sing—whatever.

As all of these [government] decisions impact on you and your finances, it pays to know what the government is doing and planning to do. You can then take steps to adjust your business accordingly.

There are some high-profile examples where government policy decisions have enraged sections of the economy to the point that the vested interests have campaigned to water down or even reverse government decisions. Some of these interventions have been at great cost to the overall setting of economic policy and, in turn, to the community.

One such case was the frenzied campaign against the mining resource rent tax by the mining companies. The tax was obviously designed to take some of the super-profits from their bottom line in an industry that is extracting and largely exporting a non-renewable resource. Unlike a factory or tourism, which can keep going forever, once the last bit of iron ore has been dug up, Australia will have no more to produce. The miners lobbied hard to reduce the tax and eventually have it abolished. Incredibly, they succeeded by arguing that the mining tax was raising a mere fraction of what it should have, and in 2014 the mining tax was abolished. In years to come, when economic historians look back and conclude that the one in 100 years mining boom should have generated a larger and longer lasting legacy for future generations, it will be the success of those fighting tooth and nail against the mining tax that will be found to be largely to blame.

Another case rather nearer to the heart of this book was the campaign of the banking industry, their financial planners and some superannuation companies to oppose government policies designed to lower fees for superannuants and improve the skill set for financial advisers. These changes were for the benefit of superannuation fund members and would have enhanced their long-run returns. Those arguing against them presented the reforms as increasing their cost of doing business and lowering their fees. This issue is still up in the air, but I suspect that eventually common sense will win and there will be a better regulated and more transparent funds management sector.

It can often be difficult to work out what the good intention of a government policy may be and to look past the campaigning from the interested sectors and other parts of the economy that will lose out if the government adopts the policy.

A good example here is the tough and well-considered decision of the Abbott government to phase out subsidies and other assistance to Australian-based car manufacturing companies. The economics of this decision were powerfully strong. Huge and costly imposts on consumers were associated with the government's forking out hundreds of millions of dollars for decades to keep a few car manufacturers operating in Australia.

The eminently sensible decision to end this funding, so the money could either be saved by the government or used elsewhere in the economy, was based on some very simple economic dynamics: Australians don't like buying Australian-made cars and have an overwhelming preference for cars made overseas. Linked to that is the fact that foreign manufacturers, on average, make cheaper and better cars than we do. Making cars in Australia for the sake of it was an expensive indulgence that was not financially sustainable.

In light of this argument, it seemed a proverbial no-brainer to phase out government financial assistance to the car manufacturing industry. But such was the emotion, vested interest and loudness of the voices of those set to lose this support that the decision copped a great deal of flack. It even fed into the more general view of some in the community that it is desirable to use taxpayer money to fund inefficient industries.

Government policy needs to make sure that other sectors of the economy are sufficiently strong to pick up the slack as the motor vehicle sector winds down.

Admittedly there are some very real and painful consequences for those working in the car industry. Here the government has to ensure that those losing out as the industry closes down receive support during their 'transition' to new jobs to ensure they do not fall into long-term unemployment. The same principle should apply to firms linked to the car industry, including those supplying parts and other components. Government policy needs to make sure that other sectors of the economy are sufficiently strong to pick up the slack as the motor vehicle sector winds down.

As you can see again in this example, we keep coming back to the virtues of a strong, growing economy.

The move to end subsidies is still progressing. The local car manufacturing industry will close in 2017. It is too early to be sure how well the government will implement the next leg of the policy dynamics — assisting those who do lose out when seeking new skills, new jobs and new opportunities.

Such are the trade-offs and competing priorities of government. When it makes economic policy decisions — whether on cars, the rate at which the age pension increases, how much universities charge you for a degree, even what medicines are covered by the pharmaceutical benefits scheme — it needs not only to keep an eagle eye on the implications for the bottom line of the budget, but also to be alert to the implications for the real economy as well as the social impact. Tough decisions by the government inevitably impact on you individually and on your business.

As for the government, in Australia the next election is never very far away. Our three-year election cycle brings us to the ballot box faster than just about any other country.

The next federal election is scheduled for around September 2016 and we can and should hope that the tone and depth of the debate on economic policy is lifted from its previous low. We should expect that both sides of politics focus on positive issues in economic management and look to the medium-term wellbeing of the economy and society and to issues of fairness and decency. This means that when voting you should judge the political alternatives on how the economy, your business and your individual financial questions will be framed over the longer run and how our society, the environment and associated matters will pan out.

When voting you should judge the political alternatives on how the economy, your business and your individual financial questions will be framed over the longer run.

During the election campaign I will be looking to all parties for an economic policy platform designed to help Australians move to high-skill, high-income jobs. To world-best public transport systems and roads. To rail, port and airport systems that allow our bulk commodities to be exported easily and cheaply, and encourage tourists to come and go in droves. To a healthier society. To sustained low unemployment. To a fantastic environment in which we are doing a minimum of harm to our planet and maybe even repairing some of the damage done in years passed. To a truly civil society in which every person can maximise their potential.

This is all idealistic, of course. But there is nothing to stop us demanding that our politicians move in that direction and cease to focus on highly emotive issues that work against sound long-run economic policy choices. It is difficult to imagine many people of any political persuasion arguing against such objectives. It is just a matter of getting our governments to focus and then deliver on them, and for people to challenge the vested interests that will do anything to protect their patch and inhibit broader and fairer progress.

The private sector and market forces have a lot to do to help us achieve these objectives. Indeed, a vibrant, dynamic, innovative and profitable private sector is vital for long-run success in any economy. That corporate success usually cannot be achieved without the contribution of the government when shaping the structural framework of the economy through its policy settings.

Various surveys over the years have suggested that voters don't mind paying a bit more tax if they can see where the money is going and as long as everyone *else in the economy, including the business sector, is paying their fair share.*

If the Australian economy is to continue its stunning record of economic growth without a recession into a 25th, 26th and 27th year, it needs policymakers to implement reforms that support business activity, efficiency and productivity. But it must do this in a fair and equitable way, ensuring that the benefits of the economic expansion do more than trickle down to those who are on lower incomes or whose opportunities are otherwise restricted. Various surveys over the years have suggested that voters don't mind paying a bit more tax if they can see where the money is going and as long as *everyone* else in the economy, including the business sector, is paying their fair share.

Proof of this was delivered with the decision of the Gillard government to increase tax — the Medicare levy, in fact — to cover a significant part of the cost of introducing the National Disability Insurance Scheme. The NDIS is expensive. When it is fully up and running it will cost more than $4 billion of government money a year to run. It is in the nature of the sector, with its propensity for expensive operating costs, that this amount will continue to rise each year on the back of rising wages and an increasing coverage of people in the scheme. The money to fund it has to come from somewhere.

The Gillard government decided that a 0.5 per cent addition to the Medicare levy would be a suitable way to raise the bulk of the money needed for the NDIS. This simple policy change was widely seen to be fair. The measure received little critical comment, other than from the small-government, Tea Party ideologues at the electoral fringe. Decent people could see the benefits and fairness of the NDIS and knew that it had to be funded via extra revenue. Thanks to bipartisan support, the Medicare levy was raised and the NDIS is now being rolled out.

Looking forward, the Australian economy faces new challenges with the end of the mining investment boom and with both terms of trade and national income growth falling. If the economic policy debate remains pitched at low-brow sloganeering, true reform is likely to be limited and the risks to the economy will be elevated. This could lead us into our first serious economic downturn since the early 1990s. If, on the other hand, common sense and policy leadership can be brought into play on the issues that will shape the Australian economy for the next decade and more, I suspect that the electorate will be happy to go along for the ride. Whoever takes the first step should have electoral support. Bold policy choices with a long-run view will mean that the economy will continue to do well.

KEY POINTS

- Government policies will impact on both your business and your personal finances.
- Tax, spending and government regulations will always set some of the important boundaries in which you operate.
- The next few years will almost certainly see a mix of tax hikes and spending cuts, so be alert to where the specifics of these policy changes will be.
- Be an advocate of good economic policy. Some recent policy shortcomings were a result of vocal interest groups shouting louder than the rest of the population, who would otherwise have benefited from the economic policy changes.

---

chapter seven
YOUR RESERVE BANK

The Reserve Bank of Australia (RBA) is probably the most powerful economic institution in Australia and is the first place you should look to for insights about the economy and financial markets. Given it is the body that sets official interest rates, its assessment of interest rate risks is of course enlightening. So when the RBA says or publishes something, take note.

The RBA releases a large amount of information on the economy on a regular basis. It is open and direct when it updates its judgements on where the economy is going, the outlook for inflation and the risks surrounding those and other forecasts.

Setting the agenda—analysis and forecasts

The RBA does not always get it right. It is, after all, staffed by mere mortals. Like the rest of us, its staff make judgement calls on where the economy has been, where it is now and where it is going. When it sets official interest rates, it is making a judgement that the level for the cash rate it enforces is consistent with its broad objectives for the economy. Like the rest of us, the RBA is often surprised by global and domestic issues that emerge unexpectedly and influence its judgements and policy settings. And like the rest of us, as circumstances change, its views (and policy settings) may also change course.

Forecasting fallibility aside, the output from the RBA is of the highest standard. When specific economic issues emerge, it throws its research efforts into uncovering the factors underscoring these trends in the economy. You just have to look at the detail of its Quarterly Statement on Monetary Policy, the transcript of the bi-annual appearance of senior RBA officials before the Parliamentary Economics Committee, the minutes of the Board's monthly meetings or speeches from RBA staff to get some penetrating and often unique insights into the economy.

Forecasting fallibility aside, the output from the RBA is of the highest standard.

When the Australian dollar is well away from fair value — for example, when it was around 50 US cents in 2000–01 or, more recently, when it was stuck above 95 US cents — the RBA produced a myriad of research pieces on what fair value for the Aussie dollar should be. It then outlined what had influenced the dollar and judged it was misaligned. It does not pretend, as do some economists, that it knows all of the factors driving markets and the economy, but it will lay out the issues it judges to be most important and rule out others it thinks are insignificant.

There has been similar deep and detailed analysis of house prices in Australia and other parts of the world. The RBA has written many hundreds of pieces covering the issue of house prices, focusing on the factors that influence prices. It forms judgements on whether or not the often emotive public discussion on 'bubbles' and affordability are legitimate.

The RBA has produced research that sets the agenda for debate in other key areas too. It has a sound understanding of things that matter to Australia such as commodity prices, the terms of trade, estimates of full-employment, inflation targeting, the current account — on and on.

Suffice to say, if you were to spend some time looking through RBA publications, you would learn a lot about how the economy works, what stage of the cycle it is at, where the risks and imbalances are and, importantly, where the policy pressures are in terms of higher or lower interest rates.

The RBA Board meets on the first Tuesday of every month except January, so there are 11 opportunities each year for interest rates to be adjusted. It can, in an emergency, adjust rates outside the scheduled dates, but this rarely happens. Curiously, over the 25 years since the RBA began announcing its interest rate adjustments, 'no change in official interest rates' has been the result of around 75 per cent of its Board meetings, which means that on average there are just three interest rate adjustments per year. That said, the RBA did not adjust interest rates at all during 2014, which was only the second year since 1990 that did not see a monetary policy change.

If you were to spend some time looking through RBA publications, you would learn a lot about how the economy works, what stage of the cycle it is at, where the risks and imbalances are and, importantly, where the policy pressures are in terms of higher or lower interest rates.

There is usually a lot of hype around each RBA Board meeting, even when the odds strongly favour interest rates being left unchanged. TV reporters effectively camp outside the RBA building, and the radio news people interview market economists with 'previews' or 'what to expect' predictions of each meeting. Everyone in the markets writes a little article outlining their views on what the RBA will consider and decide on interest rate settings. When interest rates are changed, the media coverage reaches a crescendo on why it happened and what it means.

Inflation targeting

Fundamental to the RBA monetary policy decision each month is the outlook for inflation. The RBA sets official interest rates with a view to maximising economic growth while keeping the annual inflation rate at between 2 and 3 per cent over the course of the business cycle.

But what could be better than to use the RBA's own words on the inflation target and use of monetary policy.

THE RBA INFLATION TARGET

The following is the official, quoted description of the RBA's inflation target.

In determining monetary policy, the Bank has a duty to maintain price stability, full employment, and the economic prosperity and welfare of the Australian people. To achieve these statutory objectives, the Bank has an "inflation target" and seeks to keep consumer price inflation in the economy to 2–3 per cent, on average, over the medium term. Controlling inflation preserves the value of money and encourages strong and sustainable growth in the economy over the longer term [see figure 7.1]...

This is a rate of inflation sufficiently low that it does not materially distort economic decisions in the community. Seeking to achieve this rate, on average, provides discipline for monetary policy decision-making, and serves as an anchor for private-sector inflation expectations...

The inflation target is defined as a medium-term average rather than as a rate (or band of rates) that must be held at all times. This formulation allows for the inevitable uncertainties that are involved in forecasting, and lags in the effects of monetary policy on the economy. Experience in Australia and elsewhere has shown that inflation is difficult to fine-tune within a narrow band. The inflation target is also, necessarily, forward-looking. This approach allows a role for monetary policy in dampening the fluctuations in output over the course of the cycle. When aggregate demand in the economy is weak, for example, inflationary pressures are likely to be diminishing and monetary policy can be eased, which will give a short-term stimulus to economic activity.

Source: © Reserve Bank of Australia, 2001–2015.

Figure 7.1: inflation over the long run

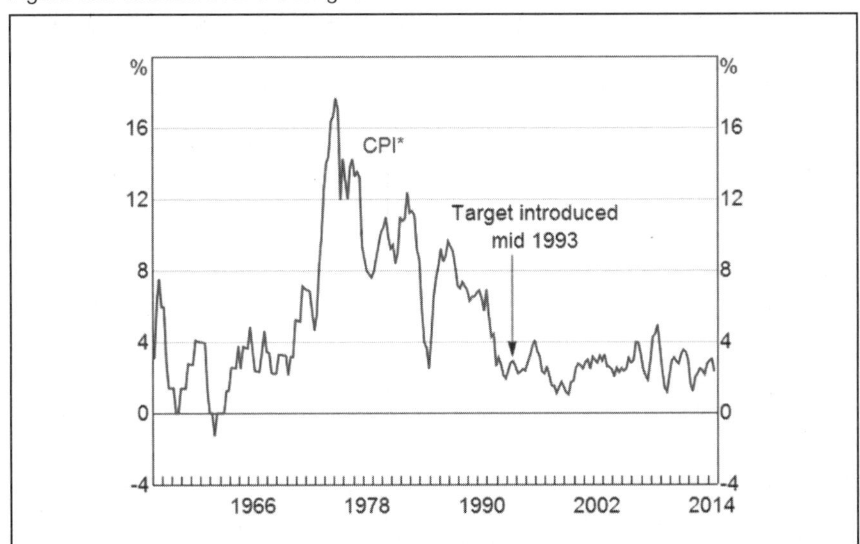

Source: © Australian Bureau of Statistics 2015; © Reserve Bank of Australia 2001–2015.

The RBA's assessment of economic conditions, including trends for the global economy, domestic demand in Australia, unemployment, wages growth and countless other issues, feeds into its judgement about the outlook for inflation. If it judges that inflation is more likely than not to stay low relative to its target and the economy is a little soft, it normally will set interest rates very low. If inflation pressures are building and look like breaking above the top end of the target band, interest rates will be set at a higher level. It is as simple as that.

As the RBA is at pains to explain when discussing this methodology and the context of the inflation target, that there are often temporary price shocks that feed into the inflation rate. A cyclone in Queensland may force up banana prices and hence the rate of inflation, as did the introduction of the goods and services tax. But these are only temporary factors and not inflationary pressures that come from economic growth being too strong.

A cyclone in Queensland may force up banana prices and hence the rate of inflation, as did the introduction of the goods and services tax.

The RBA will, in its own words, 'look through' the impact of these one-offs and focus on 'underlying' inflation, which is the inflation rate judged to be most strongly linked to demand and capacity pressures in the economy.

RBA AND ONE-OFF ITEMS

When Cyclone Yasi hit Queensland in 2011, the banana crop was all but wiped out. In the supermarkets, this meant the price for now very scarce bananas climbed from around $3 a kilo to $15 a kilo. While bananas do not have a huge weighting in the inflation rate, the quarterly rate of inflation rose 1.4 and 0.9 per cent in response to the banana price escalation, with the annual inflation rate jumping to 3.5 per cent—well above target.

With an inflexible inflation target, the RBA might well have increased interest rates to tackle this inflation breakout.

But hold on. When the next banana crop grew as the weather conditions normalised, the price of bananas fell back to $3 a kilo and the quarterly inflation rate fell to 0.0 and 0.1 per cent for two quarters, which in turn saw the annual inflation rate plummet to 1.2 per cent, well *below* the bottom of the target.

If the inflation target was inflexible, the RBA would be frantically slicing interest rates.

Clearly, it would have been wrong for the RBA to increase interest rates on the back of a banana price-inspired pickup in inflation that was always going to flow through the data when banana growing conditions normalised.

This is why the RBA focuses on underlying inflation rather than the overall headline rate. It is one of the subtleties that needs to be understood when outsiders analyse RBA monetary policy deliberations.

In terms of the bigger picture and the benefits of the inflation targeting policy regime, there is no doubt that the economy is well served by low, relatively stable inflation. It is perhaps no coincidence that ever since the RBA embraced its inflation target in 1993 under the governorship of Bernie Fraser, Australia has not had a recession. Low and relatively stable inflation is vitally important for Australia in maintaining and even building its international competitiveness. If the cost of doing business in Australia (the rate of inflation is a good proxy for this) rises at a faster pace than the costs in its international competitors (their rate of inflation is lower), then locally based firms will be less able to compete and economic activity and jobs will be more likely to go offshore at a cost to Australia. In other words, countries with persistently high inflation are usually weak in terms of economic growth and unemployment.

Low and relatively stable inflation is vitally important for Australia in maintaining and even building its international competitiveness.

What is very encouraging about the RBA inflation target is that it has bipartisan support. The target has never been seriously questioned or been a matter of policy dispute with either major political party, nor has it been raised as an issue during an election campaign since it was established in 1993. Long may this last. It means that for now this source of stability and foundation for managing the economy will remain. For your business and investments, as the RBA notes in its research and commentary, you can make your investment and savings plans confident that over the course of a business cycle, inflation will stay between 2 and 3 per cent and most likely average somewhere very close to 2.5 per cent.

HAS THE RBA HIT ITS TARGET?

Since the June quarter 1993 (the unofficial start point for the RBA's inflation target of between 2 and 3 per cent), on average over the business cycle, the following results for inflation are very enlightening.

The high for annual inflation is 5.1 per cent; the low is –0.4 per cent.

(continued)

HAS THE RBA HIT ITS TARGET? *(cont'd)*

In more than 20 years of inflation targeting, the annual inflation rate has been above 4 per cent for six quarters and below 1 per cent for five quarters, so not a lot of time more than 1 percentage point above or below the target band.

Interestingly, the inflation rate has been at or between 2 and 3 per cent—that is, within the target band—less than 45 per cent of the time. Some might query whether that is a very good success rate, but any such criticisms are completely overwhelmed by the fact that the average inflation rate since 1993 has been 2.5 per cent, slap bang in the middle of the target.

I'd give the RBA something close to 10 out of 10 for that success rate.

Other RBA functions

There is a little twist, thankfully not an important one, when one considers the wording of the legislation that established the RBA in 1959. The Reserve Bank Act 1959 requires the bank to conduct monetary policy:

> in such a manner as, in the opinion of the Reserve Bank Board, will best contribute to:
>
> 1 the stability of the currency of Australia;
>
> 2 the maintenance of full employment in Australia; and
>
> 3 the economic prosperity and welfare of the people of Australia.

Over the years, and certainly in the period since inflation targeting has been the main goal, the RBA and the Treasurer of the day (who appoints the RBA Board and oversees the RBA and its operations) have interpreted currency stability via the inflation target rather than the level of the Australian dollar. The decision to float the Australian dollar in December 1983 meant that it was always going to fluctuate in line with fundamentals with interest rates more stable. Prior to the floating of the dollar, it was the other way around, with often huge fluctuations in interest rates needed to keep the dollar at its predetermined level.

The other requirements of the RBA Act have also been interpreted, quite rightly, in the framework of maintaining and achieving this inflation target as the best way to maintain full employment and increase the economic prosperity and welfare of the people. In other words, if the inflation target is not met, it is just about impossible to have monetary policy set so that full employment and prosperity are delivered.

The RBA does a few other important things that get precious little coverage, including:

- Conducting open market operations to ensure the smooth and stable function of the banking sector
- pursuing other aspects of financial stability such as responding to financial disturbances should they occur
- managing Australia's foreign exchange reserves
- promoting efficiency and competition in the payments system, including regulating the clearing and settlement of financial transactions in the financial sector
- acting as banker to the Australian government, responsible for all aspects of the production and issuance of Australian banknotes.

These are all vitally important functions, but all usually out of the public eye—unless something goes wrong. The less we hear of the RBA operations in financial stability and the like, the better the job they are doing.

KEY POINTS

- The RBA is the premier economic body in Australia—watch carefully what it says and does.
- Monetary policy and interest rate settings are the RBA's main focus and are set in the context of a 2 to 3 per cent inflation target.

chapter eight

YOUR FAMILY

Most of us have family. Mums and dads, husbands and wives, brothers and sisters, sons and daughters. The thing is, some of these undoubtedly wonderful, lovely, caring and considerate members of your family are expensive to look after, nurture and nourish. Children cost a lot and generally don't earn an income, and it is this issue that this chapter will spend most time on. For the oldies, refer to the chapters on superannuation and buying a house.

For 18 years, and usually longer, your children will cost you money — obvious outlays cover food, clothing, health, entertainment and the like. All of these expenses will need to be factored into your weekly or monthly cost of living equation.

Today both parents are increasingly keen to undertake paid employment (often to maximise the quality of the family home they can afford to buy). But your personal finances will be severely impacted if or when you decide to have children, who will need care and supervision well into their teenage years.

For 18 years, and usually longer, your children will cost you money.

Then there are the so-called big-ticket items over and above the everyday 'running costs' of having children.

Childcare costs

Early in the child's life, child care is perhaps the most significant expense, especially when both parents want to remain in paid employment. Even with the relatively generous childcare rebates the government provides, the out-of-pocket and after-tax expenses of funding child care can be prohibitive. Which is why one parent will sometimes choose instead to stay at home to work on child-rearing while the other earns the cash. This loss of cash income for the one who works on home and childcare duties is almost always significant.

It is difficult to know how best to plan for these costs. Inevitably, the lion's share is incurred when a couple are relatively young, are probably near peak mortgage debt, have yet to reach maximum income earning capacity, and hope to have the funds to enjoy life after their the child-rearing responsibilities are completed. It is a very tough time financially, especially if one partner forgoes an income to look after a child, even for a short while.

And obviously the more children you have, the greater the cost.

There are no hard and fast rules for dealing with these financial imposts. It will depend on the cost of child care, which may be influenced by whether there are other family members, probably grandparents, who can step in and offer some after-school care. It will also depend on how much you would earn if you were to undertake paid employment. Unlike house prices and interest rates, for which the financial rules are fairly simple, these child-rearing variables will differ substantially from family to family. Not everyone has grandparents, or they may not live in the same city or be able or willing to look after your offspring. Of course, there are many single parents too.

Unlike house prices and interest rates, for which the financial rules are fairly simple, these child-rearing variables will differ substantially from family to family.

Before one partner decides to take time out from paid employment to stay at home and look after the children, consider the risk that the home duties parent may lose their workforce attachment. While a huge chunk of your take-home pay can go to covering childcare costs, by remaining in work you will probably continue to move up the pay scales and in seniority, continue to build your super, keep up with trends in your area of employment and remain engaged in a career. Time out to look after the children and these important income- and career-enhancing opportunities may pass you by.

Suffice to say, children are expensive.

As noted previously, various governments have implemented policies that alleviate at least some of the costs of child care. For many, however, these are not 'game changers' that encourage both partners to go back to paid work. The policies merely help those families who have no choice but to have their children looked after for a fee.

Governments know this is a high-profile issue in the community but will likely pay it only lip service for the simple reason that any meaningful reform to child care would come at a huge cost to the budget.

With government finances under pressure and likely to stay that way for some time to come (as discussed in chapter 6), the odds are against the introduction of more generous family payments or tax adjustments to reduce the financial cost of child care. Governments know this is a high-profile issue in the community but will likely pay it only lip service for the simple reason that any meaningful reform to child care would come at a huge cost to the budget. One merely has to look at the debacle of the Abbott government's paid parental leave scheme, which has been widely criticised as unfair, costly and unnecessarily complex.

While some small additional government financial relief is likely, I am afraid that any development in government policy relating to childcare costs for you is likely to be minimal. If child care is expensive for you, the cost to the government of covering some of these expenses for millions of parents would create a significant drag on the budget. This is why major changes are unlikely. The bottom line is you will either have to work out a way to fund it yourself, change your lifestyle so the children can be looked after or, if you choose paid employment, rely on your family to cover the times you cannot be there.

As your precious children grow up, the costs go beyond those hefty childcare costs or one parent's lost income.

Public vs private schools

The trend towards educating children in private schools has been a powerful one over the past few decades, and the increasing number of parents who choose private schools face a huge financial sacrifice. Your reasons for choosing to spend large sums of money to send your child to a private school are clearly your business. But if you do, be aware that in today's dollar terms, over 12 years the tuition fees alone will add up to around $250 000 after tax. Two children, and it becomes half a million dollars.

What if instead you put the money you would otherwise be paying in private school fees into a bank account earning even moderate interest for 12 years and send your children to the local public school. When they finish Year 12 you could hand over to your children the quarter of a million dollars saved. How would you and they feel?

Pretty euphoric, I would guess.

Would their education be any the poorer for being gained at the local public school as opposed to the private sector alternative? All the major studies on the topic suggest not. Public schools deliver an education standard at least equal to those of the expensive private school system. This is not to say, don't send your cherubs to a private school — it is your choice and you may have non-financial reasons supporting your decision. I am simply outlining the financial implications.

Public schools deliver an education standard at least equal to those of the expensive private school system.

COST OF A PRIVATE SCHOOL EDUCATION

Let's assume you plan to send your child to a private school where the annual fees are $20 000. If, instead, you sent them to a public school and put that $20 000 in the bank, with a 5 per cent compound interest rate, at the end of 12 years you would have saved, in today's dollar terms, around $300 000 (assuming that interest rates are a little above the rise in school fees). That is, for reference, close to half the price of an average house—more for a house that is below average price. Either way, it would be a chunky deposit for your 18-year-old's house purchase!

For those schools where the fees are $10 000 a year, if you placed that amount in a deposit every year for the 12 years of schooling, you would save close to $135 000 or around a fifth of the value of an average house. A very nice deposit for a house or whatever else you might wish to spend it on.

Some private schools charge even more than $20 000 a year, so you can see the price that is paid for schooling.

The issue comes down to opportunity cost. A private school education or a lot of cash?

It's your decision.

It must be emphasised strongly that not everyone can get even close to thinking about paying for a private school education for even one let alone two or three children. But as noted, from the sole viewpoint of education this matters little, given the high quality of public schooling.

And that is the good news and the legacy of a generally well funded, high-quality public school system. So if you don't have the money or the inclination to send your children to a private school, the public school system is an obvious and outstanding alternative. And even if you have the money or can scrape it together to cover the private school fees, think about how much easier life would be financially if you did not fork out hundreds of thousands of dollars on school fees.

COMPARING PUBLIC AND PRIVATE SCHOOLS

In December 2014, *The Sydney Morning Herald* reported on a range of studies into the education outcomes of students who attended public schools versus those attending the high fee paying private schools.

The most enlightening findings reported quoted Helen Proctor, an education researcher from the University of Sydney, who said quite starkly, 'There's a really widespread belief among some members of the community that their kids will do better academically at a private school but it seems not to be the case…If you're just looking at academic results, it probably isn't worth paying all that money for an elite private school'.

In an assessment of the 60 most advantaged schools in New South Wales, public schools scored above 90 in 38 per cent of their exams, on average, while the rate was 26 per cent in private schools.

When they have put in the hard slog, worked to the best of their ability and finished Year 12 with a strong university entry score, your gorgeous son or daughter will celebrate finishing school, strutting their stuff at the formals. Then along comes the next hip-pocket jolt—university fees.

DON'T TAKE THAT GAP YEAR!

A common desire for some students when they finish Year 12 is to take a so-called gap year—that is, to take a year off to do something different and postpone university for a year. Again, it is your choice, but it is worth thinking about the cost of doing so.

Let's look at a stylised example.

Two young people have just finished Year 12. They have equal abilities and achieved the same university entry score. They aim to do the same three-year degree after which they will get a job where the starting salary is around the average for university graduates in 2013, at $52 500 a year. She goes straight to university; he takes a gap year, travelling around Europe and generally bumming around home.

Let's fast forward four years.

The 'gappie' has just finished university and is about to start his career in paid employment. She has finished her first year of work, has taken home around $42 500 and is on her way in the working world with all the joys of earning an income. She has also accumulated around $5000 in her superannuation fund.

That gap year looks to have been pretty expensive from the perspective of opportunity cost, if nothing else.

After another year, the gappie has collected his $42 500 in take-home pay and now has $5000 in superannuation, but the early starter now has taken home $85 000, has over $10 000 in superannuation and has gained valuable work experience. And who will be the first to get the promotion to the $70 000 role a step or two up the ladder?

Gap years are fine, and go for it if you want to, but they are very expensive for both child and parent.

University fees

We all aspire to providing a great education for our children so they have every opportunity to achieve great things academically and in their working lives. University is a vital stepping stone to those objectives.

University fees are high and under the current policy regime are still rising rapidly. There is also a push from the government to greatly increase the interest rate that is applied to the debt that many students accrue when they choose to defer the payment of fees. For the moment the implementation of that policy has hit a few snags passing the Parliament.

It is difficult to be sure how much university fees will rise in the next few years and whether the proposal to hike the interest rate on university debt will become law, but it is safe to assume that the cost of going to university will skyrocket in the years ahead. Just when you thought education and other childcare costs might ease as your children finished school, huge university fees turn up. And if you want a university education, these cannot be avoided.

Of course, the children can accrue university debt and pay interest for the life of that debt—ouch! Talk about imposing huge costs on the younger generation. I suppose you as a parent could forget about it and not worry because your child is, after all, a young adult and hopefully financially aware when they rack up this debt, and they can pay it off once they start work.

I suspect many parents will not want their children to enter adulthood burdened with a huge university debt, especially when the benefits of buying a dwelling are so compelling.

It seems very likely that Australia will continue to move towards a US-type system where people need to start saving for the cost of university soon after their child is born. Some banks offer such university fee savings accounts in Australia now, which is probably a good business decision on their part. Parents, or grandparents for that matter, will try to make a financial contribution to reducing the accumulation of university debt so that kids can get on with life debt free when they start working.

It seems very likely that Australia will continue to move towards a US-type system where people need to start saving for the cost of university soon after their child is born.

Another issue relates to the probability that the interest rate charged on university debt is likely to remain lower than any bank loan, even if the Abbott government's now redundant plan to link it to the 10-year government bond interest rate gets through the Parliament. This may persuade some people that it is desirable to keep the HECS debt because it is cheaper to service. That option would be self-defeating once you move into the income bracket where HECS starts to get repaid, when the take-home pay of the student with HECS debt will be shot to bits. Pay it off early if possible. Be aware that the debt immediately on leaving university could well be $40 000 for a short, low-cost degree or up over $100 000 for longer, more complex studies.

And think of this dreadful scenario.

Your child does really well at school, gets into university and finishes a degree with terrific results. They are swamped with job offers and land a great job with a good income. How good is that? It is a parental dream come true. For the young adult, they have done all this brilliant study, yet they start work at age 22 or 23 with a university debt of $40 000 or more. Yuk!

But there is further grim news. Earlier chapters outlined how important it is financially to save the deposit to buy your first house and to start chipping in for superannuation as early as possible. For the young person in their mid 20s who may wish to be having a whale of a time, living early adulthood in a footloose and fancy-free way, the financial realities will be hugely challenging if they have a chunky HECS debt. Not only is their take-home pay seriously eroded as they chip away at that mountain of university debt, but saving for a deposit for that first house will be so much harder.

In simple terms, how does this young, successful person get ahead financially with a huge university debt and a desire to buy their first house?

It is tough, and something that as a parent you need to be aware of as your child gets ready to go to university.

Perhaps we will see a reversal in the trend towards sending children to private schools with parents' savings set aside to cover university fees so their children can focus on earning money and getting their foot in the door of the property market. Maybe it will be the realisation that giving your son or daughter $10 000 or more for that gap year would be better spent on covering the HECS debt when they start university on time. Or for the young person themselves, by not having a gap year and getting into the workforce earlier, they can probably make inroads into their HECS debt using the income they start earning a year before their friends who do take the gap year.

Healthcare costs

Then there are the health costs for your precious family. These are rising sharply because we are, on average, living longer and there are better and more expensive medicines and treatments available. Adding to the costs will be the probable Medicare co-payment each time a family member visits the doctor or has a blood test or x-ray. Keeping your family in good health can be expensive, and at a time when there seems to be a strong move to a more 'user pays' system when it comes to health, these costs are likely to rise. So don't get sick!

Alas, most illnesses are not a matter of choice, so we will all have to deal with these rising costs. You can make some provisions for these expenses by taking out private health insurance to complement the Medicare system, but even basic insurance costs for a family are high. It is to be hoped that our government keeps a decent safety net for when some bad luck on the health front hits your family.

To summarise, raising a family is very expensive and in many respects the costs seem to be rising as fast as, or faster than, incomes. Childcare, school and university fees, and health care have been rising at a pace above the inflation rate for some time. Available evidence suggests this trend is likely to continue in the years ahead. Just another factor to plug into your money management spreadsheet of life.

KEY POINTS

- It is expensive to have children.
- Childcare costs are a huge issue for many couples and can distort decisions about whether to stay in paid work or stay at home and save childcare costs.
- There are huge financial implications for whether you send your children to private or public school.
- Don't have a gap year — it could cost you $50 000 in today's dollar terms.
- University fees and debt are a growing issue for families and young Australians. The debt for fees is still worth accruing but try to pay it off early. Or parents: save so you can pay the fees up front and your children can start life without the burden of a HECS debt.
- Healthcare costs are growing as we live longer. Be aware that these costs are likely to keep rising rapidly in the years ahead.

chapter nine

YOUR TOUGH DECISIONS

You want it all and you want it now. But unless you win the lottery, invent the next Windows, have stinking rich and generous parents, or discover a chunk of iron ore in your backyard, you can't have it all, and certainly not now.

Realistically, to have most of what you want, you need to make choices about spending, saving, investing, relaxing and risk taking.

Home economics

Wander around any city or moderate-sized town and you will see people having a coffee, eating out, spending lots of money on food. I will avoid getting too much into home economics here, but when you go to your favourite little café and order a ham, cheese and avocado toasted focaccia and skinny flat white, you are not only paying for the ingredients that make up those delicious things to eat and drink. You are also paying for the labour of the person who makes them and brings them to your table, the electricity used in the coffee machine and toaster, the rent on the shop, the insurance for the business, the interest on the business overdraft, the water to wash your dirty cup and plate, the detergent, the cost of the coffee machine, dishwasher, the table and the chair you sit on. This is why a coffee is $3.50 or more and a nice sandwich is $10 a pop. And this is before the café owner has derived any profit so she can draw a wage and pay her personal housing mortgage, her family expenses and so on.

I hope you get the drift. Eating out, compared with eating at home, is an expensive luxury when you take into account all of these costs.

Certainly, eating out means you save time otherwise spent on shopping, preparing the meal at home and cleaning up afterwards, and it is a very pleasant thing to do. But it is also obvious to anyone who has run a household budget knows that if you buy fresh food and prepare it yourself, rather than eating out, you save a small fortune.

This little example shows how it is possible to make a tough (or maybe not so tough) choice about your hard-earned money: you can pay the café owner's rent, insurance and dishwashing powder, or you can make those yummy things at home using your own labour.

Anyone who has run a household budget knows that if you buy fresh food and prepare it yourself, rather than eating out, you save a small fortune.

The same principle can be applied to your house purchase. Buying what you think is a less desirable house in a less desirable area with a smaller and more manageable mortgage might be a tough decision, but it still probably beats renting in a 'good' area and letting the housing market and your progress towards home ownership slip for a few more years.

Car purchases

I haven't mentioned your car purchase at all, because given the themes that run consistently through this book, the argument should be obvious. Do you buy or lease a lovely but expensive car or go for an economy model, one without all the bells and whistles you will never use, but that will still get you to the same places in the same time? You could use the money you save in other areas of your life, such as paying off your mortgage a bit faster or adding a few extra dollars to your superannuation. Or even eating out because you have that spare cash. It should be obvious, but often it is not. It is frightening to see the number of highly indebted people who choose, for whatever reason, a luxury car rather than looking to their financial security through making a personal 'sacrifice' by buying a cheaper one.

COST OF CARS

Here is an illustration of the consequences of different car purchasing decisions.

Let's say you have a choice between buying a $30 000 new car or a $60 000 new car. You have the cash to pay for them outright, but what is the true cost of buying the cheaper rather than the more expensive one?

We won't even take account of running and insurance costs, which I generously assume are the same on both cars. (In reality, the expensive car will cost more to insure.)

Let's just look at the opportunity cost of the $30 000 difference. If we assume 5 per cent interest rates prevail, this means the extra $30 000 for the expensive car will cost $1500 a year or $30 a week more, just to own it and park it in the garage.

Let's also assume that over five years both cars depreciate by 60 per cent. The resale value of the $60 000 car is $24 000, down $36 000 over that time, while the $30 000 car has a resale value of $12 000, down $18 000 over that time. For the expensive car, the depreciation or cost of having the car has been $7200 a year or around $140 a week, while for the $30 000 car, the cost has been $3600 a year or around $70 a week.

Over the course of five years, the cost of choosing a $60 000 versus a $30 000 car is around $25 500, or $100 a week more than if you chose the cheaper car.

Think that might cover some university fees for the kids?

Stealth wealth

Some of this discussion reminds me of an expression I heard a lot when living in London a few years ago. Maybe it was the people we were mixing with during our three-year stay or even the area where we lived — not snooty Notting Hill or Hampstead, but the eclectic, cosmopolitan area around Herne Hill, Brixton and Dulwich. It was an expression that a number of Londoners embraced: 'stealth wealth'.

Stealth wealth was a lifestyle pursued by quite a few seemingly slightly eccentric Londoners. Many of these people were loaded financially, with high incomes and an ability to do and buy almost anything they wanted. Yet they wore inexpensive clothes and drove unpretentious cars, lived in areas and houses that were nice but not ostentatious and 'in your face'. They went about their business enjoying life but not flaunting their wealth with ridiculously expensive cars, houses and the like, even though they could easily afford them.

Having wealth but not showing off about it, and using it to maintain a great lifestyle — this is a proven way of building or accumulating yet more wealth.

Those enjoying stealth wealth, in our observation, drank expensive wines, never hesitated to go to the best restaurants, had lots of terrific holidays and lived very well. From our friendships and conversations we discovered that this lifestyle was made possible in part by keeping the appearance of financial modesty. Having wealth but not showing off about it, and using it to maintain a great lifestyle — this is a proven way of building or accumulating yet more wealth, as shown in the car example.

All this is just another way of saying, I suppose, that a lot of money is wasted on things that frankly don't matter, things we don't need, costs that could easily be avoided in everyday living. It is hardly a huge sacrifice to eat a home-cooked meal rather than paying many multiples of its cost to eat out, or to drive a $30 000 car rather than one costing $60 000.

KEY POINTS

- Most people can save money easily. When you eat at home you don't have to pay the café owner's overheads of insurance, rent and wages.
- Car purchases are another example where you can save a small fortune while achieving the same outcome — having a car to drive you around.
- 'Stealth wealth' is a nice British concept that recognises you can be doing very well without the need to show it off by living (and spending) extravagantly.

---

chapter ten
YOUR FUN

The previous chapters have all been a bit serious — about saving carefully, borrowing what seems to be lots of money for your house or business, trimming unnecessary spending and thinking about how much money you need to accrue for your retirement. 'Boring' and 'you only live once' might be the refrains after reading and digesting these homilies.

Along the way to financial security and prosperity, it is obviously important to have fun, do nice things, spend time and (inevitably) money on things you want to do that perhaps don't contribute to these primary objectives.

Check your basic spending patterns

People have many different things they like to spend any 'spare' money on. Holidays, shoes, clothes, technology, art, racehorses, concerts, restaurants — the list is almost endless.

I sometimes get into trouble for pointing out how by simply changing some basic spending patterns you might discover even nicer ways to spend your money. But I feel I need to do it anyway!

Think about this. A coffee a day from that cute café on the way to work will set you back $1500 a year — after tax. Real money that you could do something else with if you chose to make your coffee in the office. Okay, coffee is a great morning heart starter, but reducing your purchasing to one every second day would pay for two pairs of $400 shoes a year, or three lavish dinners for two at some fancy restaurant, or a couple of airline tickets to some lovely, exotic destination.

You get the drift?

This chapter makes a few points, some quirky, about spending your money on fun things. Of course, where you spend your money is your choice, be it on coffees, meals out, technology, owning pets — whatever. The following examples are merely to highlight some issues associated with spending choices that we all make every day and that we can all adjust to if needed.

Comparing costs may surprise you

We all have different perceptions of extravagance. Few people will be aware, for example, that owning a 5 per cent share in a top-grade racehorse trained by one of Sydney's or Melbourne's leading trainers costs about the same as keeping a cat or a dog.

It's true!

I am not suggesting that everyone wants to or should look to buy a share in a racehorse, or anything else for that matter. The examples that follow are about choice and perception. I can't think of too many things more wasteful than spending $400 on a pair of shoes, but then again I have dreamed of owning a racehorse, or at least a share in one, for a very long time. So once I felt that my finances were in sound shape, I leapt in. Over the past couple of years I have bought shares in a number of horses. When I tell people about this, many are aghast! 'How can you afford it?' 'Are you mad? How much does it cost?'

On top of the initial share cost, which of course is significant, I will admit that the ongoing costs are not affordable for everyone, but they are not quite as onerous as one might think. Sure, the training fees, vets, equine dental work, shoes, spelling costs, transport and the like all add up, there is no doubt about that. But from my experience, a 5 per cent share in a horse sired by Lonhro, Not A Single Doubt or Starspangledbanner, and having it trained by the likes of Gerald Ryan, Matthew Dunn or Peter and Paul Snowden, is not prohibitively expensive.

To be clear, and just to reiterate, I am certainly not suggesting that everyone go out and buy a racehorse. Or expensive shoes or an expensive watch, for that matter. Rather, the point I am making is that you should look at your finances critically and sometimes you might find it is no more expensive — and a lot more fun — to do something a bit crazy, and for me that has meant buying shares in racehorses.

And yes, I love pets too. They bring companionship and delight to the whole family. We have a gorgeous cat, Zoe, who is family in the way most cats are. There is a lot of fun in owning a loyal dog or a slightly arrogant cat. But when I have a winner at Randwick, the exhilaration is stratospheric. Even a slashing run for second in a Group 2 race at Rosehill, or a winner in a maiden race at Lismore on a sunny Sunday afternoon, is hugely exciting.

An ordinary pooch that sits by the fire at night and licks your face with unquestioning dedication costs a lot, as does your furry feline that demands Fancy Feast food, fresh kitty litter and a scratching pole. If you don't believe me, do the maths, which all dog and cat owners probably know only too well when regularly loading up the supermarket trolley with pet food, paying the vet to lance the abscess, or dropping off Fido or Fluffy at the pet hotel when the humans take a holiday.

First the racehorse.

The costs of keeping a racehorse vary a lot from month to month according to whether they are in work, racing, spelling or somewhere in between, but the total annual expenses amounts to around $2500 to $3000, or $200 to $250 a month. Recall that this is for a 5 per cent share and that this covers all expenses — feeding, training, shoes, vet, race entry, the lot. It is clearly a large amount of money but not so very much when compared with a range of other expenses I might choose to incur each year.

Now look at the cost of your friendly family dog.

In any given year, the cost of owning a dog is, wait for it, close to $3000 — sometimes even more. That estimate is based on the following costs.

Dog food is not cheap. Being conservative, the tins of meat, the dry crunchy pellets plus an odd treat of a bone cost an average of around $3 a day. Sometimes the food is much more than this, sometimes a little less. This adds up to around $1100 a year.

Then there are the dog hotel fees when you are away for work or holiday. Assuming 20 days a year away (some people take more holidays than this, of course) at about $30 a day, depending on the establishment, this adds up to a further $600 a year.

Then you may need to take account of grooming. A mobile dog shampoo and tidy-up is at least $70 a pop. Dog stylists suggest a visit every six weeks, but let's be conservative and push that out to a wash and blow dry, trim and groom, once every two months—so six grooms a year and there is another $420.

By this stage your pet is costing you over $2100 a year.

The variable and unknown costs are for the vet, including vaccinations, worming tablets and the like. But ask any dog owner and invariably these vet bills will total at least a few hundred dollars a year. Given that it costs around $400 a year for dog insurance that covers nothing like 100 per cent of vet bills, let's go for something like $500 a year for vet visits, on average.

Now we are pushing $2600 a year or about $50 a week, which is more or less the costs of a 5 per cent share in a quality racehorse.

So, in terms of ongoing out-of-pocket expenses, the cost of a share in a racehorse is about the same as owning a dog.

I suppose we should add to the pet's bills the cost of collars, leashes, treats, bowls, flea powder, blankets, the amortised cost of the kennel and the like, and $3000 a year is looking a fair guess for owning a dog. If you have what might be called an 'energetic' dog, you may have other costs such as garden maintenance, gates and fences. And as much as you love your dog, you do have to pick up the poo. This last impost of course is hard to put a value on.

So, in terms of ongoing out-of-pocket expenses, the cost of a share in a racehorse is about the same as owning a dog. But here is where it gets interesting, at least financially. A critical difference between owning a pet and a racehorse is that a dog or cat is unlikely to earn you any money. A horse just might.

I have purchased my shares in racehorses through a syndicating company, Dynamic Syndications. They buy the horses as yearlings at the annual sales and nurture them for several months before selling shares in each one. The minimum share is 5 per cent, and when the vet and training and other bills start rolling in all costs are divided by 20.

In Dynamic Syndications' long experience, around 90 per cent of the horses they have syndicated have earned prize money. The average of that prize money over a racing career is over $70 000, although it must be acknowledged that a few standout horses such as Reward For Effort, He's No Pie Eater and Atomic Force have been hugely successful, which boosts this average. Winning a Golden Slipper or a Cox Plate or the Magic Millions or the Blue Diamond boosts the average, just as when James Packer walks into a room the average wealth of the people in the room jumps.

And yes, some of the horses have not won races or been financially viable for one reason or another, which is one of the obvious risks one takes when deciding to buy a share. You may not win any money at all.

Around three-quarters of horses syndicated by Dynamic Syndications have earned more than $50 000 over their career in today's dollar terms. Recall that for a 5 per cent share, this prize money is divided by 20. If the horse races for, say, five years and wins around the average, I can expect to 'get back' around $500 a year in prize money, lowering the net cost of owning the horse further. Suddenly it is starting to look like it is cheaper to own a share in a racehorse than to own a pet.

Who would have thought that!

Money well spent? That's your call!

Let's look at spending on entertainment. Many people love going to the movies, concerts, the opera, the theatre or the latest world-class exhibition at the art gallery. It is not uncommon for a family to spend $2000 each year on these wonderful forms of entertainment. The joy from attending these can be almost limitless, which is why so many people spend their hard-earned money in this way. But is the cost of these tickets dead money or is it money well spent?

A few thousand dollars each year no doubt provides a good dose of stimulation and entertainment when you embrace the delights of *Carmen, Mary Poppins, Summer of the Seventeenth Doll, Hamlet,* a One Direction concert, or a quirky mix of Hollywood blockbusters and fringe movies. Most who spend their hard-earned cash on immersion in the arts will no doubt think it money well spent.

But is it? As soon as you walk out of the theatre, all you have are memories of a great performance, perhaps some brief inspiration and the satisfaction of knowing you have enjoyed some top-notch entertainment. There is nothing more. Now think of someone who loses $2000 a year betting on horses. Could it be that, like the opera goer, the punter spends $2000 to experience brief entertainment and long, glorious memories? Isn't it like all other expenditure on experiences, such as the theatre or holidays?

Certainly, it is foolish to part with money you can ill afford to spend, be it on a mobile phone, a car, a business, concerts or indeed gambling. Like most other issues flagged earlier in the book, it is about choice. Have a gap year, by all means, but see how much it costs. Go to a private school and again, simply note the cost. Bet a few dollars on the horses or go to the opera, and simply note how much it costs.

For me, the experience of going to the races and punting a few dollars is every bit as entertaining as listening to Beethoven's Fifth or Taylor Swift or watching *The Third Man*, even if I do lose dough on the hot favourite.

Seeing the horse I backed hold on for a win, or watching it flounder in the heavy-going for last place, creates highs and lows that mirror the emotional seesaw of watching a Shakespearean classic or the latest James Bond thriller. Some people are addicted to opera, have season tickets to the theatre year in and year out, queue up for hours so they can see the Rolling Stones in concert, and spend many hundreds of dollars for these pleasures.

If this is you, by all means do it and have a great time. Good luck to you. For me, I am off to the TAB with a few dollars in my pocket. I reckon I will have more fun backing the dish-lickers at Dapto, trotters at Melton and the thoroughbreds at Bendigo and Randwick than someone watching *Il Trovatore* or *Swan Lake*, catching Bruce Springsteen or reading *The Book Thief*. But if these things appeal to you, of course, do it! It is your choice.

KEY POINTS

- Spending money on fun or things that are nice to do is great — you are probably doing it now.
- Be alert to areas where money leaks out of your savings so you can compare and evaluate the potential costs and pleasures of different experiences.
- Excessive spending is never good for your financial health, so avoid it. That said, we all need to think about our discretionary spending, whether we choose to spend money on holidays, concerts — or punting on the horses.

chapter eleven

YOUR NEGATIVE GEARING

One very popular way you might make money through investing is via negative gearing, which simply means having the interest you pay on debt used for investment purposes as a tax deduction from your annual income.

Negative gearing is a reasonably straightforward investment strategy. The following illustration shows roughly how it works.

What is negative gearing?

If you borrow $100 000 for investment purposes at an interest rate of 5.5 per cent, the annual interest cost of $5500 is deducted from your taxable income. For those in the top income tax bracket, that reduces your annual tax liability by approximately $2700. That is a decent saving for investments funded through debt. Where the debt is, say, $500 000 for an investment property, the tax savings are more substantial, even in the current low interest rate environment. Obviously, the more you borrow by this means, the greater the tax deduction you have each year and the greater the leverage you have for your investment portfolio.

The objective of investing that money is to earn an income flow on the investment, and to make a capital gain over time.

It is easy to see why the scheme is growing in popularity so strongly. Around half of all new mortgage finance at the end of 2014 was directed at housing purchases for investment purposes. It is extraordinary to realise that, in effect, by negative gearing you are getting other taxpayers to pay a large part of the interest on your debt, and that they are directly helping you with your asset accumulation.

This is of course why the policy is problematic—it is unfair. Low and even middle income earners are less likely to be inclined or indeed able to borrow large sums for investment purposes, so they do not get to engage all that often in negative gearing. With the progressive income tax structure in Australia (as you earn more money, you move into a higher income tax bracket on those earnings), even the low and middle income earners who choose to negatively gear their investments get less of a tax deduction or subsidy. This is simply because they are in a lower income tax bracket than high income earners and, accordingly, their tax deductions are much smaller for each dollar of interest paid.

In effect, by negative gearing you are getting other taxpayers to pay a large part of the interest on your debt, and they are directly helping you with your asset accumulation.

Be that as it may, within the negative gearing strategy there are some curious issues regarding the way Australians choose to allocate the funds they borrow for investment purposes.

There is a massive and overwhelming bias in favour of investments funded by borrowings to flow into residential property versus relatively trivial amounts negatively geared towards buying shares (margin lending). According to data from the RBA, the amount outstanding on margin lending for shares is tiny, at around $12 billion, or less than 1 per cent of the value of shares traded on the ASX, while credit outstanding for housing investment purposes stands at around $500 billion, which is close to 10 per cent of the value of all dwellings in Australia, including those that people own to live in. A casual observation would suggest this is a massive mismatch given how well regulated and sound the Australian stock market is and how sound the bulk of the listed companies are, and given how high house prices appear to be. These figures also suggest at least some downside risks in the housing market if the investor side of housing demand slows or, in a worst case for prices, starts to fall.

What is even more staggering has been the change in the investment flows from borrowed money in the aftermath of the GFC.

House credit since the GFC

Before the GFC exploded global markets and the world economy, the value of margin lending, or borrowings for the purchase of investing in stocks, was $42 billion (December 2007). This means that since then the value of margin lending has fallen by around 70 per cent, a staggering fall in what is otherwise a very popular asset class — shares.

In terms of housing credit for investment purposes, the value of borrowing outstanding at the end of 2007 was $290 billion. This means that in the subsequent seven years, credit for dwelling investment purposes has risen a stunning 70 per cent.

Looked at another way, in 2007, before the GFC, negative gearing for housing was seven times larger than for stocks. Some seven years later and borrowing for investment housing is more than 40 times larger than for stocks. In terms of the money involved, credit for housing investment purposes is up over $200 billion in that time, while for stocks margin lending is down $30 billion.

These are massive shifts in what are two huge asset classes for virtually all Australian investors and may well help explain the relative performance of the asset classes over that time.

Credit for housing investment purposes is up over $200 billion in that time, while for stocks margin lending is down $30 billion.

Investors who have been behind these quite spectacular changes in borrowings have generally made the correct asset allocation. Since the end of 2007, house prices have risen more than 30 per cent Australia wide while the ASX was around 15 per cent lower in early 2015 as this book was going to print (5400 index points for the ASX200 compared with 6340 points at the end of 2007).

In other words, over seven years there has been a 30 per cent capital gain for houses versus a 15 per cent capital loss for stocks.

Stocks vs property investment

I am not about to offer specific investment advice (I am not qualified to do so), but I would like to note that economic and financial market history offers many lessons. One of those is that there are cycles, which by definition means substantial fluctuations in valuations for different asset classes over time. Linked to that is the reality that no asset class outperforms or underperforms forever. There are times when some investments weaken and then are cheap, and other times when they are expensive and then enter a period of relative price weakness.

Linked to that obvious statement is the point that when one, still soundly based, asset class has been weak over a reasonably long time frame, it almost always will rebound over the medium term. Yet another point, to labour the issue, is that when a particular asset looks and feels expensive, it probably is expensive and it is likely due for a few years of either falling prices or underperformance relative to other assets. In 2015 that asset is housing.

In a way, these observations about the market are truisms but they are still worth noting. A hard-headed reality check on bandwagon or herd investing frequently sees markets overshoot and then correct lower. Before then, investors often get in way too late in the cycle, usually after the bulk of price gains have been made. When the market turns lower, the herd often takes fright and sells after suffering losses because they fear losing more. They often sell near the bottom.

A hard-headed reality check on bandwagon or herd investing frequently sees markets overshoot and then correct lower.

If I were to hazard a guess on capital growth of stocks versus residential property over the next five to seven years, and it is a guess of course, my money would be firmly biased towards stocks outperforming housing. And by a considerable margin, maybe even reversing the 30 per cent housing gain versus the 15 per cent stocks loss of the past seven years.

Think, if you will, of a scenario in which the proportion of borrowed money for investment in stocks relative to housing returns to the 2007 level—that is, seven times. Even on what would be a very conservative assumption of 3 per cent growth in housing credit over the next few years, by 2018 margin lending for stocks would need to rise to over $80 billion. This is unlikely, certainly, but even a trend in that direction would no doubt support share prices if that were to happen.

When it comes to investing, as the very old and frequently ridiculed saying goes, it is essential to buy when prices are low and sell when prices are high.

While margin lending for stocks is currently in the doldrums, for whatever reason, it would be no surprise to see a jump once investors gain confidence in the market or when the housing market cools and the bandwagon effect of investing in property slows down and investing in stocks heats up.

When it comes to investing, as the very old and frequently ridiculed saying goes, it is essential to buy when prices are low and sell when prices are high. On the stocks versus housing investment decision for the next few years, this would suggest a high probability of some stock market outperformance over housing at least in terms of capital gains.

But beware!

Politics of negative gearing

Before you get too excited about negative gearing and the opportunities for a nice boost to your superannuation fund, including by having other taxpayers pay up to half the interest bill of your investments, negative gearing is vulnerable to a policy change from your government.

Both sides of politics are looking at negative gearing changes to help move the budget back towards surplus. The fact that tax deductions for negative gearing are expensive for the government and the issues of fairness and equity, raised above, mean there is a reasonable possibility that in the next year or two or three negative gearing will be phased out or abolished. If you are heavily leveraged, the tax benefits to you could be lost.

The politics of negative gearing and the huge financial benefit for those using it for investment purposes will mean the politicians will tread warily before phasing it out or abolishing it. Given how many taxpayers — and voters — have a vested interest in its retention, getting rid of negative gearing is undoubtedly one of those policy decisions mentioned in chapter 6 that, while fair, sensible and fiscally prudent, suffer from 'too politically hard' syndrome. No doubt, there would be very vocal and well-directed campaigns launched by the vested interests that would lose out from such a change.

Given how many taxpayers — and voters — have a vested interest in its retention, getting rid of negative gearing is undoubtedly one of those policy decisions that, while fair, sensible and fiscally prudent, suffer from 'too politically hard' syndrome.

Tax policy speculation aside, negative gearing and borrowing to leverage your investment portfolio clearly benefit high-income earners substantially. Those with some accumulated wealth that can be used as collateral to ramp up the leverage, whether their investment destination is housing, other property or shares, will continue to do so while the law supports it.

KEY POINTS

- Negative gearing is a great way to boost leverage for your investments and have other taxpayers subsidise the interest cost of your borrowings.
- The overwhelming investment bias towards residential property and away from stocks has been the right decision to date, given the capital gains and losses in each asset class.
- There is potential for stocks to outperform residential property over the next few years.
- Beware of the risk that negative gearing may soon be phased out.

---

chapter twelve
YOUR WORLD

Earlier chapters have touched on the global economy, the rise of Asia and the general weakness in the industrialised world in the aftermath of the GFC. For Australia, the importance of these global economic and market trends has been apparent for many decades. In recent times, it has been the rise of Asia that has been most significant for our economy and individual prosperity.

From an economic perspective, Australia has the good luck of being geographically close to Asia. We produce many of the goods and services increasingly demanded by Asia's booming economies. And, very significantly, we generally have had political leaders who over many decades have recognised and acted to develop and build our links with many countries in our region.

What is also important is that Australia has welcomed two-way trade and investment flows, building economic ties in the region, including through the formation of the Asia-Pacific Economic Cooperation forum. Australia has also been a driver of the agenda of the Group of Twenty (G20), the main focus of which is economic policy.

We generally have had political leaders who over many decades have recognised and acted to develop and build our links with many countries in our region.

This chapter aims to develop some of these themes and touch on the still very important part of the world economy outside of Asia and the role it plays in driving the Australian economy and markets. It should be no surprise that your business, your job and your investment plans can be driven by events in small to medium-sized economies as well as the big ones, and especially those with which Australia trades and invests heavily.

The global economy

How big is the world or global economy? A few basic facts here are quite enlightening.

According to the World Bank, global output of goods and services—world GDP—was around US$80 trillion in 2014. Recall Australia's share of this is around US$1.5 trillion, meaning that a lot of other countries produce a lot of GDP.

The 27 countries that make up the major economic unit of the European Union as a whole account for around 24 per cent of global economic production. That means, quite obviously, that what happens in the European economic and policy space matters to the world. The recession and deflation currently permeating Europe means a quarter of the world economy is stagnant, not adding much to demand, and it has economic policy settings that continue to influence bond, stock and currency markets.

Moving away from the EU, let's look at some specific countries. Table 12.1 lists the 10 largest economies in the world and their share of global economic output.

Table 12.1: 10 largest economies and their share of global economic output

Country	Share of global GDP (%)
United States	22
China	12
Japan	7
Germany	5
France	4
United Kingdom	4
Brazil	3
Italy	3
Russia	3
India	2

Source: World Bank, reference year 2013.

It is interesting to see that the contribution of any individual country to the world economy quickly falls away to what are small contributions. The biggest three countries, namely the US, China and Japan, account for around 40 per cent of global GDP, but the tenth on the list, India, accounts for just 2 per cent of global output. Recall that these numbers are in US dollar terms.

For Australia, and for you, these figures should be revealing. What, for example, do we know about the economy of Brazil, the seventh largest in the world and a major competitor to Australia in terms of agriculture and natural resources? Not much, I would assume. Or the huge array of countries that are not on that table but are important to us economically and strategically, even though their contribution to world GDP is relatively small? These include the likes of Indonesia, South Korea, Mexico, Spain, New Zealand and Thailand, to name a few.

Crucial linkages in a globalised world

There is an interesting and crucial linkage that helps to explain how the EU, which accounts for only 5 per cent of Australia's exports, is so important to our economic performance. Given that South Korea, for example, is just as significant as an export destination and is taking a growing share of our exports, should more of our attention be directed to Seoul?

Not necessarily, and it would be a grave mistake to downplay the importance of Europe. The EU matters to Australia much more than our direct trade with it, and this is because of its standing as a major buyer of Chinese exports. The EU is the largest export market for Chinese manufactured goods. When the economy of the EU is weak, as has been the case for the past year or two, its demand for Chinese manufactured goods will be stagnant and its growth close to non-existent.

With our focus here on Australia, 'so what?', you might ask.

The link comes through the materials, energy and other commodities used in the production process for the goods China manufactures and exports. The lower the demand for Chinese manufactured goods from the EU, the lower the output of goods in China, which in turn means less use of raw materials, including the energy resources that China buys in huge volumes from Australia. This, in turn, means the volume of materials and the price paid for them is likely to be weaker.

This showed up clearly during 2014. As the EU economy remained weak, lurching in and out of recession, the Chinese economy slowed to record its weakest GDP growth rate since the early 1990s. The price of iron ore, coal, oil, natural gas and other metals went into free-fall. With that, Australian firms producing those materials had their profits cut. They wound back output further and any new production that might boost investment was all but stopped. Some of the higher-cost producers of these commodities fell into genuine financial difficulty.

The linkages in an increasingly globalised world are strong and growing.

But what of other global events, such as the threat of the Russian government defaulting on its debt? Or Greece or Italy breaking away from the Eurozone? Or the Swiss central bank cutting interest rates to minus 2 per cent? Or the change of government in India in 2014? These are just a few examples of things that are happening in the world economy and global financial markets that impact on the Australian economy, even indirectly, and that can have significant implications for our businesses and investments.

There is only so much you can fit into a few minutes of TV or radio news, or information that is 'click-bait' for online media, when you are up against George Clooney's wedding, outrage at some right-wing politician or other inconsequential flim-flam.

None of these critical developments got much coverage in the Australian media, even though each was important in its own way. The nightly news still reported the market moves but not why they happened. There is only so much you can fit into a few minutes of TV or radio news, or information that is 'click-bait' for online media, when you are up against George Clooney's wedding, outrage at some right-wing politician or other inconsequential flim-flam.

All of this is to underscore the point that the global economy and markets matter, even if some of these issues appear to be of relatively minor direct relevance to Australia.

The world economy matters increasingly because of the massive structural changes over the past 50 years, especially in globalisation. This is how the GFC spread and came to impact on Australia and how businesses have to change if they are to survive, let alone grow. Globalisation means we all have greater access to a wider array of goods and services produced all over the world, which is great for us as consumers. It is great if you are a producer of one of these items as your potential market expands from just 24 million Australians to the whole world. But it may not be so good if you are in a business contending with these new competitors.

The world economy matters increasingly because of the massive structural changes over the past 50 years, especially in globalisation.

The problems that led to and exacerbated the extent of the decline in economic activity as a result of the GFC—including poor regulation of banks and mortgages, excessive risk taking in an unstructured competitive finance and insurance sector, and poor macroeconomic policy more generally—were not significant issues in Australia. We did not have the crazy excesses in housing. We did not experience the significant economic or regulatory policy errors or the unconstrained competitive free-for-all that smashed the US, UK and parts of Europe and that led to the most significant economic downturn since the 1930s Great Depression. Yet, as the GFC unfolded, the Australian economy slowed sharply, moving to the cusp of recession. Just about everyone, but especially Treasury and the RBA, were forecasting a recession for Australia. The unemployment rate rose, inflation fell and government revenue was smashed, leaving the budget in substantial deficit. The onset of the GFC saw Australian interest rates fall to levels never before seen. The Australian dollar dropped 40 per cent and share prices were cut in half, even though Australia did not have the structural problems that dogged many other countries.

So how did this happen?

Globalisation in banking and financial markets meant that a bank in the United States could issue a bond on behalf of a client that was bought and held by a bank in France, which used that bond as collateral on a trade it undertook in the futures market after it hedged the foreign exchange exposure with a bank in the United Kingdom, which loaned many multiples of the money via derivatives trading with a fund manager in Japan for mortgages in Ireland, and the Irish bank also raised leveraged capital from the Australian financial markets in which your superannuation savings were invested... and so on. You see?

This illustrative chain of linkages was good while it lasted. In a sense it allowed the free flow of capital and meant that the world economy grew, with lots of liquidity and plenty of appetite for the more risky investments; paradoxically, though, these links turned out to be at the core of the problem when the pass-the-parcel of credit and money ended. The reality of the derivatives market was much more complex than this, but the key point here is that when the music stopped, the banking sector, financial markets and the global economy were pretty much as weak as the weakest link in this chain. When one link broke the whole system came tumbling down, dragging Australia and everyone else with an advanced banking sector down with it.

When the mortgage market in the US buckled under the weight of rising interest rates, poor regulation and outright fraud, it not only started to pole-axe the US economy but brought down the banking, insurance and funds management industries around the world too. As we have seen throughout the post–World War II period of economic history, when the US goes into recession, the rest of the world economy suffers. And this time around the problem was compounded by increasingly interdependent financial links.

Globalisation and the impact of global economic conditions matter too when, for example, there is a sharp move in US stocks. At face value, it is hard to grasp why a 2 or 3 per cent point fall in the Dow Jones Industrial Average of US stocks on a particular day is automatically followed by sharp falls in the Australian stock market. This is especially the case when there is no local economic or corporate news to support such market weakness, or indeed when the local stock market news is positive. It is especially disconcerting to observe the sharp price fall of, say, retail company Woolworths, which drops when the overall US stock market has a sharp fall, even though there is no adverse news on Woolworths or related data on retail trading released in Australia.

Economists have an explanation for this phenomenon. The link is a little subtle, but it is quite real. When you realise that a sharp fall in US stocks could be the start or the continuation of a more enduring decline, it could mean trouble for the US economy. This would hurt overall global GDP growth and would therefore lower demand for Australian commodities. This, in turn, if sustained, would hurt company profits in Australia and hence employment and consumer spending—and so the linkages flow. Understanding them helps explain why our market almost inevitably follows sharp moves in the US, whether up or down.

This familiar example relating to the US stock market is well established, but the pressures on Australia are likely to change slowly but very surely change in the years ahead.

Understanding [the linkages] helps explain why our market almost inevitably follows sharp moves in the US, whether up or down.

With the spectacular expansion of the Chinese economy and its steady move to internationally tradable financial assets (foreign exchange, bonds, stocks and the like), it is increasingly clear that movements in China's GDP, announcements from the People's Bank of China (the country's central bank) or significant moves on the Shanghai stock exchange will have a growing influence on other global markets, and especially Australia.

To some extent this is already happening. News about the Chinese economy is increasingly monitored globally, but especially in Australian dealing rooms. Unlike most European and US economic data and policy moves, which happen overnight in the Australian time zone, Chinese economic news is usually released when the Australian markets are open for business and fully staffed. While the data in China are not always reliable, they are all that economists, traders and even policymakers have to rely on to judge developments in China. When there is a surprise GDP result, an unexpected dip in industrial production or a shock reading for the export and import data, you can be sure the Australian dollar and stock market will react.

CHINA'S GDP DATA

Following is an extract from a column I wrote for Business Spectator *in 2012.*

'When I was working in Treasury a few years ago, a colleague told the story of his official visit to China. He was speaking to his Chinese counterpart in the economic forecasting section and was marveling at the accuracy of the economic forecasts of the Chinese government. He said to his Chinese friend, "Your forecasts are remarkably accurate. For GDP and inflation you are never out by more than 0.1 or 0.2 percentage points. Quite often, you are spot on. How do you do it?"

'Without an overt hint of discomfort or irony, the Chinese economist answered: "John—not only do we make the forecasts, but we also compile the data."

'This background is important in judging the true momentum of the Chinese economy and, with it, global growth.'

Reading economic and market trends

All of which leads me to the next point on how best to judge world economic and financial market trends so as to get a feel for the outlook over the next six months to a year. If the Chinese economic data are not all that reliable, how else can you tell what is happening there and more broadly in the world economy?

There are dozens if not hundreds of organisations that produce forecasts for the major countries of the world and for global GDP, inflation, interest rates, currencies and the like. To be frank, given the inherently uncertain nature of economics, financial markets and policy changes, those forecasts are not that useful. While some forecasters are better than others, no one has a record for producing consistently accurate economic and market forecasts. No one.

Analysing and interpreting major economic trends is made all the more difficult by the fact that the data published by each country's statistical agency are not always accurate and are inevitably revised, which can lead to very different economic interpretations. Also there can be a long lag between the end of the time period being monitored and the release of the data. In Australia, for example, the GDP data for a given quarter are not published until more than two months after the end of that quarter; the June quarter GDP data will not be released until the first week of September, and when those data are eventually released there is near certainty that the recent history will be revised.

While some forecasters are better than others, no one has a record for producing consistently accurate economic and market forecasts. No one.

This means that when you sit down to look at your business performance and opportunities or investments and the like, relying on less-than-reliable forecasts is hazardous, as is waiting for hard data to be released, because this is often slow or the information is simply not accurate.

All is not lost when it comes to judging the economy, though. There are alternative indicators to the official hard economic data and various forecasts that are a reliable and timely gauge of global economic conditions. These indicators are commodity prices.

Whether for oil, corn, copper, soya beans, natural gas, coal, iron ore, pepper, coffee or tin or any of the myriad of commodities that are traded within global financial markets, the broad swings in commodity prices say a lot about any imbalances between supply and demand in the global economy. They can give an excellent read on the risks unfolding in the economy well before any country produces its GDP, labour force or retail sales reports.

If, for example, there is a sustained period of weakness in the prices of a broad range of commodities, it is safe to conclude that global demand is weakening or there is excess supply or production of those items. When there has been no obvious surge in supply or you are able to cross-check the commodity price fall against some other economic indicators (the stock and bond markets, for example, which are also traded daily, and even some of the hard economic data), and if they are also suggesting economic weakness, it is reasonably safe to conclude that the global economy is weakening or slowing.

What makes commodity prices all the more appealing as a barometer of the health of the global economy is the fact that commodities are traded every day. Anyone can see the price of oil or wheat or soya beans at any stage and put today's price level in the context of recent trends. If there have been price falls for a large number of commodities used in industrial production (oil, coal, copper, iron ore, gas and aluminum), for example, then it is safe to conclude that global manufacturing output is weakening. Which means there could be issues ahead for the Australian economy, your business and your investments.

For a quick snapshot of unfolding trends in China specifically but the global economy more generally, focus on commodity prices.

In looking at commodity price trends, there are a few traps to be wary of. Most commodities are denominated in US dollars—oil is X US dollars a barrel, iron ore is Y US dollars a tonne and gold is Z US dollars an ounce. This means that sometimes the X, Y and Z values of commodities change because the value of the US dollar has changed.

What makes commodity prices all the more appealing as a barometer of the health of the global economy is the fact that commodities are traded every day. Anyone can see the price of oil or wheat or soya beans at any stage and put today's price level in the context of recent trends.

In other words, when looking at commodity price trends, don't fall into the trap of mistaking a change due to a US dollar movement for one due to a fundamental demand or supply issue. You can look at trends in commodity prices in euros or yen or, as the RBA prefers, Special Drawing Rights, which is a basket of currencies (see figure 12.1).

Figure 12.1: RBA Index of Commodity Prices

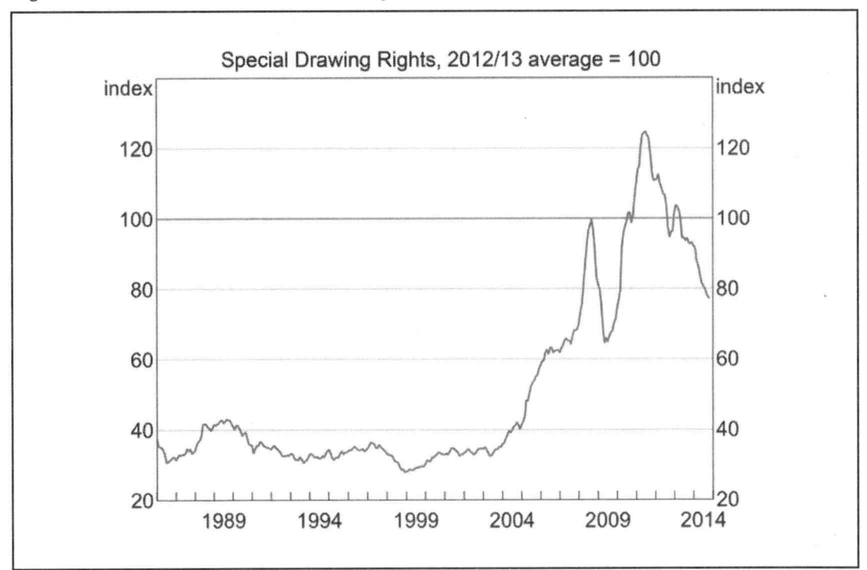

Source: © Reserve Bank of Australia 2001–2015.

WHAT ARE SPECIAL DRAWING RIGHTS?

According to the RBA, 'Special Drawing Rights are used as an international reserve asset to settle transactions between countries and help balance international liquidity. The value of the SDR is calculated by the International Monetary Fund (IMF) on the basis of a weighted basket of four currencies: US dollar; euro; Japanese yen; and UK pound. The IMF publishes the value of the SDR each day in terms of US dollars and the Reserve Bank of Australia provides an equivalent value in Australian Dollars'.

When valuing changes in commodity prices, the use of SDRs rather than just the US dollar gives a truer reading on price trends as it largely overcomes the issue of currency fluctuations.

A final aspect of the global economy to note is that the value of exports makes up around 20 per cent of Australian GDP, while the value of imports comprises a further 20 per cent or more of the economy.

Exports matter

For economic growth, exports and therefore world economic conditions do matter. How much iron ore is bought by foreigners and the price they pay for it, together with tourism, education, wheat, wool, coal and wine and all other exports of both goods and services, are critical for the Australian economy. If, for whatever reason, foreigners stopped buying our raw materials or cut back on their holidays and university spending in Australia, our economy would clearly be the worse for it.

The importance of exports can be illustrated by the fact that as a share of the economy, they are four times larger than all spending on new housing construction plus alterations and additions to existing dwellings. We get carried away by a boom or a bust in housing construction, which is fair enough, but a big swing in the export sector has an impact on bottom-line economic growth that is much more powerful than all of our housing construction activity.

The importance of exports can be illustrated by the fact that as a share of the economy, they are four times larger than all spending on new housing construction plus alterations and additions to existing dwellings.

Recognising the importance of exports matters too. And like many areas in economics, there are vitally important linkages back to the value of the Australian dollar exchange rate, the efficiency and productivity of our local businesses that are in the export space, and even issues like having low and stable inflation, which is an essential aspect of maintaining Australia's international competitiveness. It is why these issues are almost always hot policy issues.

During 2014, the RBA complained that in its judgement the Australian dollar was overvalued. This meant the exchange rate was higher than would normally be the case given the fall in commodity prices, the deterioration in the international trade deficit, the slowing rate of

GDP growth, the level of Australian interest rates relative to the rest of the world and confidence in the management of the Australian economy. A lower Aussie dollar clearly benefits the economy's bottom line via the internationally traded sectors: we would receive more dollars for our exports; our exports are cheaper to foreigners, who of course pay in a foreign currency; and local businesses that compete against overseas firms are better placed to expand and prosper.

An example of a local sector that competes directly with imports is locally based tourism, which lost out badly when the exchange rate was high. It was cheap for Australians to travel to Hawaii or California for a holiday, so the tourism sector in Queensland or Tasmania, for example, missed out when we headed overseas knowing our dollar would buy more than a US dollar. Now think of the cost of that trip to the US with the exchange rate at, say, 80 US cents — it becomes 20 per cent more expensive, and suddenly the fly-drive holiday around Tasmania or the trip to Noosa and Port Douglas is relatively cheaper.

Given the impact of the world economy on Australia, it remains critical that our policymakers get our house in order. If we remain productive, with a strong and diverse economic base, the resulting build-up of domestic resilience will help us withstand at least part of the impact of a big global economic swing. The lead into the GFC illustrates the benefits for Australia of having a well-structured economy when the external economic shock hit.

Given the impact of the world economy on Australia, it remains critical that our policymakers get our house in order.

Discussions on productivity, while critically important for the domestic economy, are about Australian industry, agriculture, financial services and all other parts of the economy maintaining and building their international competitiveness so the Australian economy can grow. Competitive tax rates, well-regulated industries and a vibrant, skilled and flexible labour market are all vital for Australia's long-run economic success, not just based on local factors, but so Australia can compete with our increasingly dynamic trading partners and international competitors.

Imports enrich our lives

The other important aspect of the global economy is the supply of goods and services that we Australians buy and consume via imports. Every day we consume and rely on imported products. These range from cars, to clothes, oil, computers, electronic goods, holidays in France, movies and champagne and many thousands of other items. It matters to us and those selling these items how much we pay for them and our access to these goods, because imports enrich our lives. This is why the reduction in trade barriers is so important. With low or no trade barriers our export products have easier access to foreign markets. At the same time imports arrive in Australia at the lowest possible price, so it works both ways. Which is why it remains critical that our economy and businesses operate at peak efficiency and competitiveness.

It matters to us and those selling these items how much we pay for them and our access to these goods, because imports enrich our lives.

And the less we as consumers pay for things in a world with lower and fewer barriers to trade, the higher our living standard.

Imports are a good thing but the critical point is that we have the productive capacity to generate enough of our own economic activity, income and exports to be able to afford those imports without persistently large deficits on international trade. Generally, Australia has done this for many years although with the commodity supercycle now coming to a crashing end, the next few years could well see the re-emergence of large and increasing trade and current account deficits. We might also see a return of debate on the issue of the level of foreign debt, which in recent times has been a sleeper despite the fact that it has recently hit a new record high.

In a nutshell, then, the world economy matters to us because of the linkages between export and import trade flows, financial market trends and our general economic wellbeing and confidence. These trends will undoubtedly impact on your business, your superannuation funds and even your mortgage interest rate. So watch for changes in overseas economic conditions and financial markets. They might, and indeed probably will, have an impact on you — whether you like it or not.

KEY POINTS

- Trends in the global economy are vitally important for Australia, so watch what is happening.
- Globalisation will only make these links stronger.
- Commodity price trends are a reliable indicator of global economic conditions, so watch for changes in prices to get ahead of changes in global growth momentum.
- Exports are a huge part of the Australian economy, which is another reason why global economic activity is vitally important to Australia.
- International trade boosts economic growth and therefore our personal wellbeing, which is why it is important to try to lower barriers to trade.

AFTERWORD
BEWARE OF ADVICE AND BE FLEXIBLE

When it comes to the economy, your business, your superannuation and basically everything to do with your money, there is just one more absolutely vital issue to consider.

Treat all advice, tips, and investment and savings strategies with healthy scepticism.

This does not mean you should ignore all advice. On the contrary, there are some very clever people out there who can help you with all matters relating to business, economics and finance, and listening to them can be very fruitful.

Those without an agenda or barrow to push are clearly more useful to you than those merely spruiking their latest offering or making big economic and financial market calls for the sake of publicity. You may recognise this latter type, with their 'House prices are set to drop 40 per cent' or 'We are on the edge of the next global recession' or 'Buy stocks now, you cannot lose' hype. Unfortunately the media love this stuff and therefore give such claims undue attention. There are some dreadful advisers and, worse still, dodgy ones who frankly do not have your best interests at heart.

So beware.

When it comes to the big decisions on borrowing for a house, looking at a plan to buy into or expand your business and, importantly, where to invest your hard-earned superannuation money, never act on the spur of the moment. Do your homework, get a second opinion, think and ask questions about fees, transactions costs, flexibility and tax.

Question the story of the self-proclaimed market 'guru' who insists the economy is particularly weak and vulnerable and is heading for a recession, but who bases his authority on having got one forecast right several decades ago. Watch out for the headline-grabbing economist who makes a spectacular claim so he will be noticed by the media herd. Think, is that stock recommendation from your broker really that sound? What about the bank helping you to restructure your loans — have they got it right?

Worst of all are those who are always either perpetually gloomy or perpetually upbeat, regardless of circumstances. Persistently negative Dr Doom type people are next to useless, because they say the market is overvalued when it goes up and then scream, 'I told you so, and it will still fall further!' when it reaches the bottom of the cycle. For them it is never a good time to buy a house or stocks. So too with those — mainly stockbrokers, in my observation — who almost always say now is the time to buy stocks.

Better to listen to those who try to call a cycle, who note that we are near a turning point, higher or lower, and who change their view according to the changing circumstances. But even then these cyclical analysts and forecasts can be wrong with the timing and order of magnitude of their predictions.

It is vital to remain flexible, to be alert to the fact that the fundamental underpinnings that impacted on your decision last year on your debt, investment or business plan can, and almost inevitably will, change and when it does you too should change. Who would have thought that the Aussie dollar would ever trade at $1.10 to the US dollar? Who would have predicted interest rates would ever fall this low? Who would have thought the Australian economy would be impacted so severely by the free-fall in the terms of trade? Who would have thought that Australia could go 24 years without a recession?

Odd things happen in economies and financial markets. This means flexibility is a vital aspect of financial and business management.

I wonder where all these and other variables will be when we get to 2020. Will the Aussie dollar be back at 50 US cents with mortgage interest rates at 8 per cent? Will the ASX have returned to 2007 levels and beyond or will it be floundering at 4000 points or lower? And house prices … that thorny issue. They look sort of expensive now, but they may remain expensive for all of the reasons mentioned earlier in the book. Will the government finally claw back that budget surplus that it has been craving, and who will be Prime Minister when it does?

Flexibility is essential because your government may introduce unexpected policy changes, or a new government may have a different policy agenda, or there may be a new global shock on oil prices, or a market move may trigger a sharp change in the level of interest rates or the value of the dollar.

In economics, there are more surprises than certainties, particularly over a longer run time frame.

Don't be complacent or set in your ways because, after all, it is your money we are really focusing on. Maintaining an 'I've always done it this way' attitude to running a business or managing your own investments is probably the worst thing you can do. Things will change, and so should you. Holding dud investments or sticking to an obsolete strategy will cost you a lot of money and heartache.

There is no doubt that being alert to all aspect of your finances will yield financial rewards, whether through negotiating and paying a lower interest on your debt, earning higher returns or paying lower fees on your investments. Being one of the early ones to become aware of changing circumstances in the economy is possible, and certainly desirable. Changing course on your strategy before everyone else realises the changes are needed is the stuff of financial success. So be aware and flexible, keep an open mind, search out information diligently, and you will almost certainly be better off financially than those who take a passive approach.

INDEX